50 of Tel Aviv's
Most Intriguing Streets

THE LIVES
BEHIND THE
NAMES

Photographs by Ziv Koren | Text by Miryam Sivan | Curated by Ellin Yassky

gefen גפן
publishing house בית הוצאה לאור
JERUSALEM • NEW YORK Est. 1981

Archival Photo Research: Lily Yudinsky
Cover Design: Leah Ben Avraham/Noonim Graphics
Typesetting: Estie Dishon
Original design concept: Lori S. Malkin Design

Front cover: Allenby Street, where the Carmel Market and Nachalat Binyamin Street meet (see p. 63). Photo by Ziv Koren. Insert: Vintage Tel Aviv poster. Alamy Stock Photo/World History Archive (see p. 62, top right).
Back cover: Busking acrobats at a red light at Rokach Boulevard. Photo by Ziv Koren (see p. 123).

ISBN: 978-965-7023-19-8

1 3 5 7 9 8 6 4 2

Gefen Publishing House Ltd.
6 Hatzvi Street
Jerusalem 9438614,
Israel
972-2-538-0247
orders@gefenpublishing.com

Gefen Books
c/o Baker & Taylor Publisher Services
30 Amberwood Parkway
Ashland, Ohio 44805
516-593-1234
orders@gefenpublishing.com

www.gefenpublishing.com

Printed in Israel

Library of Congress Control Number: 2021909268

CONTENTS

ACKNOWLEDGMENTS

Why have we produced this book on *50 of Tel Aviv's Most Intriguing Streets*?

Tel Aviv and other Israeli cities are unique almost worldwide in that every street name commemorates the life of an important person in Jewish or Israeli history — a scholar, rabbi, Zionist, politician, philanthropist, or statesman. We hope to bring these important people and their streets to life.

What is the genesis of this book? I remember sitting for many years at a café on Lilienblum Street, reading the daily Israeli newspaper and wondering who Lilienblum was and who were Arlosoroff, Ibn Gabirol, and Rothschild. It was clear that the commemorative streets in the exciting and dynamic city of Tel Aviv made for the concept of a book! I set out to put together the best team to create *50 of Tel Aviv's Most Intriguing Streets*.

Our powerhouse team includes the following individuals:

- Ellin Yassky, PhD, who made aliyah to Israel in 2012 after a thirty-year career in publishing art books with an emphasis on Jewish art and art history, heads our team.
- Miryam Sivan, PhD, our writer, is the American daughter of Israeli parents who has lived in Tel Aviv for many years and teaches literature at Haifa University and writes fiction and nonfiction books.
- Ziv Koren, the most exciting and dynamic Tel Aviv photojournalist, is known by everyone in town and throughout the world for his social and political documentary photography.
- Lily Yudinsky, an expert in Israeli archives, a visual researcher, and archival producer for more than twenty years.
- The entire Gefen Publishing House team, led by publisher Ilan Greenfield along with project managers Daphne Abrahams and Shiran Halimi, senior editor Kezia Raffel Pride, and designer Estie Dishon.

THIS BOOK IS DEDICATED TO the memory of Marcia B. Saft, writer, journalist, and amazing wife and mother, who was my collaborator on this project and specifically in choosing the list of intriguing streets. Unfortunately, she did not survive to see the project completed.

Tel Aviv, the first new Jewish city in a millennium, is an exciting, an ever-changing international and growing cosmopolitan, world-class metropolis reflecting a true mosaic that is emblematic of the Jewish people, its energy, and its history.

Our team has brought that mosaic to life on these pages. We hope you enjoy this journey through Tel Aviv's streets and history, and the making of an exciting future.

Stephen J. Saft
(An American Jew who loves Israel, the Jewish people, and the ever-changing mosaic called Tel Aviv!)

AS CITIES GO, TEL AVIV is young – just over one hundred years old. It's a place where people work hard and play hard. Infused with hope and vitality from the get-go, this city exudes creativity, fun, and ingenuity. It's also a business center, full of opportunities. Israel's second-largest city suffers no identity crisis. It knows who it is, celebrates itself, and keeps an eye on the future at all times.

In 1909, when sixty-six Jewish families decided that Yafo (Jaffa) had become too crowded, they looked north to the sand dunes and orange groves. Little did they know how quickly their small new neighborhood would develop into a city of nearly half a million people with thousands of streets, buildings, trees, and traffic jams. The society and neighborhood, originally known as Ahuzat Bayit ("Homestead"), adopted Menachem Sheinkin's suggestion in 1910 and changed its name to Tel Aviv. A prominent Zionist activist, Sheinkin, among the community's original families, took his inspiration from Theodor Herzl's 1902 novel, *Altneuland (Old-New Land)*. The novel had recently been translated from German into Hebrew and made reference to Tel Aviv, an ancient city cited in Ezekiel 3:15. *Tell* is an archeological term referring to a hill. This is the "old" part. *Aviv*, which means the spring season, is the new. Tel Aviv, then, is the ancient hill of spring, a place that expresses the past and a people's modern revitalization.

Yet the renamed Tel Aviv was neither the first nor the only Jewish settlement outside of Yafo. Neve Tzedek was established in 1886, Neve Shalom in 1890, Kerem HaTeimanim in 1906, and there were others. Eventually, all these neighborhoods became part of Tel Aviv, as did Yafo in 1950. But none of these other neighborhoods had Tel Aviv's original agenda – to become an innovative urban environment with space, light, and gardens. There would be museums, concert halls, theaters, and cafés

Late nineteenth-century tinted postcard showing the abundant orange and date groves of Yafo.

Cover from a JNF and Joint 1954 calendar highlighting Jaffa oranges, a beloved Israeli export.

The auction for the lots of Ahuzat Bayit in 1909, captured by photographer Avraham Soskin. Sixty-six founding families of Ahuzat Bayit met on the beach, north of Yafo, on the land bought from the Jiballi Vineyard. Akiva Aryeh Weiss, head of the Ahuzat Bayit Society, led the lottery. Numbers of the lots were written on one group of white and black shells, with the names of the families written on another. Lots were pulled by a child.

along the beach and boulevards where people would sip coffee and exchange ideas. There would be indoor plumbing and electricity in homes and lighting on the streets. When the Scottish urban planner Patrick Geddes laid out a west-east boulevard-centered master plan for the city in 1925, it featured these principles. The city council, with Meir Dizengoff at its head, eagerly adopted the plan.

Buildings were built; gardens and trees from a variety of countries were planted. As the population grew, more streets were paved, more houses built, and more trees planted until the borders of the city reached beyond the Yarkon River to include residential neighborhoods to the north and northeast. Today, Tel Aviv is considered the country's most

cosmopolitan city and one of the most exciting cities in the world. It is home to a wealth of museums, art galleries, libraries, theaters, concert halls, parks, gardens, and a virtual culinary cascade of restaurants, pubs, and cafés, including being a world capital for vegan cuisine. When you throw the Mediterranean Sea on the western boundary into the mix, you have a year-round water sports/beach recreation culture as well. Thanks to the founders' early vision, in 2017 Tel Aviv was cited by the World Economic Forum as one of the greenest cities in the world, with approximately five thousand trees per square kilometer!

This honorable mention rests alongside an earlier urban achievement. In 2003, the United Nations Educational, Scientific and Cultural

Patrick Geddes's city plan for Tel Aviv and its city of gardens, as submitted in 1931. This plan, which changed significantly over the years, does not envision the northern environs of the city nor an inclusion of Yafo. His plans were officially approved in 1938.

Organization (UNESCO) identified the unique architecture of Tel Aviv's "White City" neighborhood as a World Heritage Site, claiming that as home to the world's largest collection of Bauhaus and International Style buildings, it is of "outstanding universal value." Again, this is the new.

The old, alongside this abundance of modernism, is Yafo – an integral part of the city's essence and its physical, cultural landscape. One of the ancient world's important cities, Yafo is cited in the Bible numerous times and brings together the East and West, the three religions devoted to this land: Judaism, Christianity, and Islam. Over a million international tourists visit Tel Aviv-Yafo every year. They come to see the ancient and the new, the religious and the secular; they come to eat, drink, dance, and discover the streets of Israel's version of the city that never sleeps.

A word on street names. Historically speaking, most urban streets were identified by the kind of work done on them (Glassblowers' Street or Metalworkers' Street or the like) or because they were located next to a natural or built landmark. Yet there have always been streets named after and by people in power. Today the protocol governing street naming varies from place to place, but one thing is recognized by all – street names tell a story.

In 1910, of the six original streets of Ahuzat Bayit, five were named for people linked to Zionism and Jewish history: Herzl, Rothschild, Lilienblum, Ahad Ha'am (Asher Ginsberg), and Yehuda Halevi. HaShachar (the dawn) was the one exception. This street was named after an important nineteenth-century Hebrew-language newspaper dedicated to Jewish national independence. By 1925 there were 150 streets in the city for the almost quarter-million residents, and twenty years later there

were another 350 streets that needed naming. At first, all street names were discussed and voted on by the city's residents, pending approval of the town council. Many of these street names honored early Zionist writers, thinkers, and activists who helped realize the dream.

In order to catch up with the city's exponential growth, the city council's cultural committee took over the work of choosing names. This change also ensured that the story of Zionism and biblical connections to the land were highlighted. Tel Aviv was the first city in the country to have so consciously chosen its streets names, thereby displaying its political message on every street sign and corner. Menachem Sheinkin summed this up succinctly when he claimed: "It is necessary to imprint [Tel Aviv] with the seal of the idea of the [Jewish] revival, which is the main reason for its coming into existence. We will do this by means of

A 1932 aerial view of Tel Aviv, looking north from Allenby Street, shows a new urban mecca poised very much toward the future.

Left: *Descriptions of Yafo Port appear as early as the book of Jonah. For more than seven thousand years, it has been an active port of entry to the Land of Israel for all peoples. It was the main port of Palestine until the opening of Haifa Port in 1933. This late nineteenth-century image shows how life in Yafo relied upon the sea; small boats skirt the large rocks, casting nets to pull in the freshest fish.*

the names we will give the town and its streets; and these names will be with us forever."

In contrast to other Israeli cities in which the majority of streets are named after plants (with olive as the most popular, followed by grapevine), in Tel Aviv nearly all the streets are commemorative, named after people who have left their imprints on the nation and country: writers, thinkers, scientists, fighters, biblical figures, religious leaders, and politicians.

Sometimes streets were named after prominent individuals while they were still alive, as with Dizengoff, Bograshov, Bialik, Ahad Ha'am, and Allenby. Sometimes the naming of a street prompted a clash of personalities, such as this heavy-fisted example. In 1922, American immigrant Meir Shapira bought some land and built his home between two lanes off of King George Street. Then he put up signs calling the lanes after himself and his wife. Dizengoff (who twelve years later would have his own large street) rejected Shapiro's desire for immortality and

Opened in 1956, the vibrant saltwater Gordon Pool is a Tel Aviv institution. This 1960s photo predates its modern renovation, but then and now the pool lies smack on the shores of the Mediterranean. Here, city residents learn to swim and let loose with the family after a hard day's work.

commanded that City Hall name the lanes two shades of Anonymous: they are now called Simtah Plonit and Simtah Almonit (*simtah* meaning alley, and Ploni Almoni being the Hebrew equivalent of "John Doe").

This is not the only instance of renaming in the city. Renaming existing streets is a political and cultural phenomenon throughout the world. After Israel achieved its independence, many streets honoring British figures were renamed after Jews. King George was one of the few left untouched, having earned his place of pride in the city by lending a hand to the Zionist dream of return. He was sovereign when the 1917 Balfour Declaration was drafted and signed. Yet there were moments when residents opposed renaming. In the 1980s when the municipality wanted to honor former mayor Chaim Levanon by renaming University Street in Ramat Aviv after him, the neighborhood objected. Yet the people in government prevailed, and Levanon Street it is.

Tel Aviv's street names are a walking guide to the historical and ideological agenda of this city, which is both unique and yet in synch with the national story of return. One can also see historical biases by what is missing: namely women and Arabs. Of the 940 commemorative street names in Tel Aviv, only forty honor women, and only a handful celebrate important Arabs in the city's history, even though more than half the population is female and 6 percent of the city's residents are Arab. As a contemporary bastion of progressive values, Tel Aviv recognizes this imbalance, and in the newer parts of the city, such as Ramat Aviv and Ne'ot Afeka among the many other neighborhoods founded in the 1950s, street names of women and contemporary scientists, politicians, and artists can be found. The city has a waiting list of more inclusive names, and with the ongoing establishment of new streets, Tel Aviv will expand its story to include more women and Arabs, Ethiopians, Russians from the late twentieth-century immigration, and other members of the Tel Avivian community who have contributed to their city and country.

The book is divided into six sections or neighborhoods, which is intended to give the reader a general sense of the city's layout. Though the Mediterranean Sea hugs the city entirely from north to south, we

For decades, Café Nitza at 40 Allenby Street was popular with artists, bohemians, and families. It was a favorite spot for Polish immigrants arriving in the country in the 1950s and the unofficial headquarters for Yiddish theater actors. This mid-1960s photograph shows the café's typical daytime crowd.

decided to give the beach its own section with a few of the prominent streets that mark this fabulous geographical asset. The center here also includes what is referred to as the Old North, not to be confused with the neighborhoods north of the Yarkon River that continue to grow in size and prominence. Downtown is the cradle of this exciting urban landscape, and the southern neighborhoods fill in the fabric that link the metropolis to Yafo, the ancient part of the city.

CENTER

THE CENTER OF THIS CITY-ON-THE-GO showcases Tel Aviv's most prominent and exciting features. Starting at the green band of the Yarkon Park in the north, and running south to bustling Allenby Street, here is where you'll find the shopping, culture, businesses, and pleasures Tel Aviv is world famous for. This is also where your eyes will feast on the more than four thousand examples of the world's most extensive collection of 1930s Bauhaus buildings, many of which have been dramatically renovated since the White City was designated a UNESCO World Heritage Site. Boulevards lined with royal poinciana, *Ficus*, and jacaranda trees run east from the beach, providing beauty and sea breezes among the white plaster buildings. The center is where the 1925 urban master plan drawn up by the innovative Scottish geographer Sir Patrick Geddes is on full and proud display.

Tel Aviv's most important cultural, commercial, and civic institutions are located in the center: Habima National Theater; the Tel Aviv Culture Palace (Charles Bronfman Auditorium); ZOA House; Tel Aviv Museum of Art; Beit Ariela Municipal Library; Tel Aviv Performing Arts Center (Golda Center for Performing Arts) with the Cameri Theater; Israel Opera; Beit Lessin Theater; Tzavta Theater; Tel Aviv City Hall and Rabin Square; a government building; the Azrieli Center with its dramatic circle, square, and triangle towers; plus a multitude of smaller galleries, shops, and boutiques bursting forth on all the streets, with a nearly endless choice of eateries to satisfy appetites during culture and shopping breaks.

The center of the city is also famous for its many parks. From the Yarkon Park to Habima Square, from the ever-popular Tel Aviv Port to Rabin Square, and on to the new hip Sarona complex, with many smaller gardens and squares in between, this urban area provides residents and visitors with a rich variety of public spaces in which to enjoy moments of quiet, beauty, shade, and recreation.

One of Tel Aviv's more than four thousand Bauhaus buildings from the 1930s. Many in this area of the city, a neighborhood called the White City, have undergone dramatic renovations according to UNESCO's strict World Heritage Site guidelines.

CHAIM ARLOSOROFF STREET

WHEN CHAIM ARLOSOROFF WAS MURDERED on the Tel Aviv beach in 1933, the splits in the Zionist movement deepened. He had just returned from Germany, where he negotiated the Transfer Agreement with the Nazis; it was assumed that members of an extreme right-wing group, the Union of Zionist Rebels, murdered him in response. He was despised for his commitment to regional cooperation with Arab leaders and for working with and not against the British on Jewish immigration to Israel. To this day his murderers remain unknown.

Arlosoroff was born in the Ukraine in 1899 but grew up in Germany. For him, the terms of the Transfer Agreement were reasonable: it would allow Jews to emigrate from Germany, and while they would still have to pay high taxes in order to transfer their funds abroad, they would have the option of designating some of that money to purchase German goods that would then be sent to Palestine. Because the agreement broke the Jewish boycott of German products, it upset many people. Yet history has shown the wisdom of this agreement, which enabled more than sixty thousand German Jews to come to Palestine from 1933 to 1939, doubling the Jewish population and bringing vast sums of money into the country to buy land, start communities, and fund industry.

While studying for his doctorate in economics at the University of Berlin, Arlosoroff became a leader in the Young Worker Party, an anti-militaristic Zionist socialist organization. In 1919 he published *Jewish People's Socialism*, his manifesto for the Jewish community in Israel, which married socialism and nationalism. Though secular, he looked forward to the day when biblical land laws, such as the sabbatical year, would once again be a part of Jewish life.

The Dan Bus Company (once a cooperative) was founded in 1945, though as early as 1909 it provided public transportation for the burgeoning Tel Aviv community. The Dan Bus Garage was housed in a 1934 Bauhaus building.

From Tel Aviv's earliest days, the wide boulevards perpendicular to the beach were filled with trees and shrubs. The Garden in the City pleased the eye and improved the air quality – then, and especially now.

Chaim Arlosoroff (1899–1933)

Busy corner showing off some of the new – and newly restored – buildings changing the city's urban landscape. Street-level stores and cafés cater to pedestrian traffic, while towers that climb into the sky provide stunning views.

During Arlosoroff's first visit to Palestine in 1921, riots broke out in Yafo, and Jewish neighborhoods were attacked. He then understood that Jews had to accept the Arab community's concerns and began working for Jewish-Arab cooperation. Voices on both sides of the ethnic divide were unhappy with this. But it is fitting for his character and beliefs that at the young age of twenty-seven, Arlosoroff represented the Palestinian Jewish community at the League of Nations in Geneva. Later, when he became political director of the Jewish Agency, he worked with the British government, hoping they would allow more Jewish immigration and support a Jewish national homeland.

Eventually the British let him down. Faced with increasing anti-Semitism in Europe, Arlosoroff claimed that Jews had to do whatever was necessary to save Jews, even if it meant upsetting the British.

His premature death at age thirty-four was a great shock to the community. They had difficulty accepting that a Jew might have assassinated a Jew and that ideology might have been more important than a human life. A grieving crowd of close to 100,000 people escorted his coffin to its burial in Trumpeldor Cemetery in Tel Aviv.

Arlosoroff Street is a broad, tree-lined street that runs from the beach to the Savidor Central Station for train and bus travel on the eastern edge of Tel Aviv. Beautiful residential homes and larger institutional buildings run all along it.

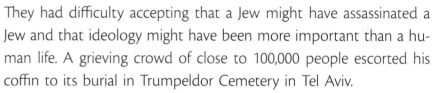

In front of a state lottery booth encouraging people to "take a chance," a man prays with ritual phylacteries courtesy of a Chabad emissary – business as usual amidst the typical backdrop of bicycles, cell phones, and old Ficus trees.

MENACHEM BEGIN ROAD

"EVEN WITH ALL THE TROUBLES and problems, *Am Yisrael chai!*" So said the complex and fiery Menachem Wolfovich Begin. Born in Poland in 1913, he came to British Mandate Palestine in 1942 as a soldier in the Polish Armed Forces and decided not to return to Europe to fight the Nazis under British command but to stay and fight the British for Jewish independence. It didn't take long for him to become the leader of the Revisionist underground movement, the Irgun Tzva'i Leumi (National Military Organization, abbreviated "Etzel"). After they bombed the King David Hotel in Jerusalem in 1946 and killed ninety-one people, tensions escalated between the Irgun and the Haganah, the military defense organization that eventually evolved into today's Israel Defense Forces (IDF). For years Begin lived under assumed names and with disguises. He feared assassination or imprisonment both by the Haganah and the British, who put a £10,000 price tag on his head.

Once the State of Israel was created in 1948, Begin lived openly again and immediately formed the right-wing Herut Party. Winning fourteen seats in the country's first Knesset elections, Begin became a vocal and active opposition leader. In 1973 his party's clout increased when two smaller parties merged. Now they had 39 out of 120 Knesset seats and a new identity: the Likud.

In 1977, Menachem Begin sent seismic waves through Israel's political landscape when the Likud won an overwhelming majority in the national elections. With characteristic zeal, he promised and implemented an economic transformation that shifted policies away from decades of socialism and that embraced capitalism as critical to the country's development. Begin was also the first prime minister to reach out to Jews from Arab countries, to the ultra-Orthodox, and to working families in the periphery. Jewish settlement in the West Bank was another value close to his heart, and his government invested heavily in housing and infrastructure there.

At the same time, in 1977, Begin responded positively to Egyptian president Anwar Sadat's proclamation that if invited, he would come to Jerusalem to discuss peace with Knesset members. That momentous visit led to the Israel–Egypt Peace Treaty. Menachem Begin, Anwar Sadat, and American president Jimmy Carter each received a Nobel Peace Prize for this work. Begin is quoted as saying, "The difficulties of peace are better than the agony of war."

Keenly aware of the historical suffering of the Jews and the recent European Holocaust, in 1979 Begin ordered the Mossad: "Bring me the Jews of Ethiopia." And they did. Thousands of Ethiopia's Jews were airlifted to Israel during Operation Moses. And with the same sensitivity to Jewish survival, in June 1981 Begin ordered the destruction of Iraq's

A vibrant young Menachem Begin makes a speech in the 1940s to his followers from one of the curved Bauhaus buildings hugging Zina (Dizengoff) Square. The balconies are filled with people listening and watching the crowd in the roundabout below.

nuclear reactor. Officially condemned by many countries, the operation was nonetheless unofficially seen as necessary.

In 1982 Begin approved Operation Peace for Galilee. The severe political and ethical repercussions of what became known as the First Lebanon War, along with Begin's wife's death, prompted him to resign in 1983 as prime minister and to retire entirely from public life. He died in 1992 and was buried as he had requested next to his wife in the ancient cemetery on the Mount of Olives. More than seventy-five thousand people attended his simple traditional funeral.

Menachem Begin is remembered for his modesty, his honesty, his blazing passion, and his vision of an Israel inclusive of all Jews. The important north-south Menachem Begin Road, previously Petach Tikvah Road, links working-class and industrial parts of southern Tel Aviv to middle-class residential neighborhoods in the city's center and north.

Today landmark buildings such as the International Style Citrus House (first steel-frame construction in the city, completed in 1938), new commercial towers, transportation hubs, government and military headquarters line Begin Road. The square, circular, and triangular towers of the Azrieli Center that define Tel Aviv's skyline are there, and the HaShalom transportation hub is a mere block away. From a two-lane, tree-lined street to an eight-lane commercial artery, the story of Menachem Begin Road parallels the exponential growth of Israel's city that never sleeps.

On Independence Day, patriotism runs so high that even residential towers under construction get in on the act. These long flags draped down the buildings' façades (see the narrow blue and white strips) are here to pronounce and celebrate Israel's robust growth.

At the busiest intersection of Begin Road, the three iconic Azrieli Towers – a square, a circle, and a triangle – peek through the roof of the modern pedestrian bridge and escalator connecting the Azrieli Mall and HaShalom transportation hub.

DAVID BEN-GURION BOULEVARD

"IN ISRAEL, IN ORDER TO be a realist, you must believe in miracles." David Ben-Gurion made this observation in an interview with CBS News in 1956 after beginning his second term as prime minister of Israel. A powerhouse of a man, often titled "the founder of the modern state," Ben-Gurion knew firsthand how the stuff of dreams was spun from hard-knock realities.

Early on in his career, Ben-Gurion emerged as the leader of the Jewish community in Palestine. He headed the pre-state Labor Zionist Party and the Histadrut, the labor union it founded. Ben-Gurion deeply believed that a new society needed a new economy formed from the working class. He was a leader in two pre-state Jewish paramilitary groups: Hashomer and the Haganah, which he helped establish. When Ben-Gurion became chairman of the Jewish Agency and the Histadrut's representative in the World Zionist Organization in 1935, he extended his impact way beyond the borders of the country, influencing the global Jewish community as well.

Born David Gruen in Poland in 1886, Ben-Gurion was raised to be a Zionist and attended a school run by his father. His commitment to Hebrew and socialism started early in his life, so by the time he came to Palestine in 1906, he was more than ready to take on the tasks of "the dream." He worked in numerous agricultural settlements, including Sejera (today Ilaniya) and Degania, the country's first kibbutz.

During World War I, the Ottoman authorities deported Ben-Gurion. He spent the war years working for the Zionist socialist cause in New York, where he met and married his wife, Paula. He returned after the war, during the British Mandate period, as a soldier in the Jewish Legion, a unit of the British Army founded by Ze'ev Jabotinsky. The oddness in this is that that it wouldn't take long before the right-wing military positions of Jabotinsky would clash harshly with Ben-Gurion's more centrist opinions when it came to working with British authorities and

Workers' housing in Tel Aviv was built using Bauhaus principles of clean, utilitarian lines, small gardens, flat roofs (for washing and hanging laundry), and individual balconies. This housing complex, photographed in 1937, is located on the corner of Keren Kayemet Boulevard (now Ben-Gurion Boulevard) and Ben Yehuda Street.

In 1936, children plant trees in honor of Tu b'Shevat, the Jewish holiday of trees. In those days, Ben-Gurion Boulevard was known as Keren Kayemet Boulevard (Jewish National Fund Boulevard). The name was changed in 1974.

in response to Arab violence against Jewish communities. The apex of this ideological clash was seen on the beach of Tel Aviv when in 1948 Ben-Gurion ordered the Haganah to open fire on the *Altalena*, a ship carrying Jews – among them Jabotinsky's protégé, Menachem Begin – and arms for the battle against the siege of Jerusalem.

Just as he had before the Declaration of Independence, Ben-Gurion continued to consolidate power after the state's creation. He was both prime minister and defense minister in the years 1948 to 1954, and then again from 1955 to 1963. Under these roles, he was able to bring all the paramilitary organizations, including his own Haganah and Begin's Etzel, under the leadership of the Israel Defense Forces. On the civil front, he ordered the establishment of many new towns and cities, the building of the national water carrier, the moving of the Knesset and other government offices to Jerusalem to establish it as the country's capital, and the in-gathering of Jews from Arab countries.

In 1970, at age eighty-four, Ben-Gurion left Jerusalem and politics behind for good and retired to Sde Boker, his kibbutz in the desert, giving himself a well-deserved retirement. As he had done his whole life, Ben-Gurion used himself as an example. He lived in a humble worker's apartment and called for other Jews to join him in making the desert their home.

Ben-Gurion Boulevard is a broad street that runs from the beach to City Hall. Its gorgeous island in the middle of the traffic lanes is filled with bike paths, benches, corner kiosks, playgrounds, picnic tables, and old tall trees that provide beauty and shade. This boulevard was renamed to honor Ben-Gurion after his death; for almost forty years he had a house at number 17.

One of the numerous corner kiosks that have popped up in the middle of the luxuriously green boulevard that buffers the pedestrian and bike lanes. Excellent coffee, sandwiches, and pastries are available as well as the usual comfortable hangout.

ELIEZER BEN-YEHUDA STREET

THE MAN WHO DEVOTED HIS entire adult life to the revival of spoken Hebrew was born Eliezer Yitzhak Perlman in Russia in 1858. Eliezer Ben-Yehuda hebraized his name in line with his vision of making Hebrew the language of the home, the school, the street, of children, of lovers, of shopkeepers, of everyday life and holy practices alike. At age three, Ben-Yehuda learned to read Hebrew. Exposed to secular writings at a later age, he was motivated to widen his knowledge, which included learning French, German, and Russian. He later went on to study the Middle East at the Sorbonne University. In Paris, he read *HaShachar* (The Dawn), an early Hebrew-language newspaper that inspired him. And then he met a man from Jerusalem who spoke to him in Hebrew. For him, this was proof that it was possible to draw the language off the page and into the mouths and ears of modern Jews. Ben-Yehuda moved to Ottoman-ruled Palestine in 1881, believing that "the Hebrew language can live only if we revive the nation and return it to the ancestral land."

His plan met with opposition from the ultra-religious community, who insisted that the holy language not be tarnished by daily concerns.

This Bauhaus-inspired building shows off the rounded intersection of Ben Yehuda Street and Mendele Mocher Seforim Street (Mendele the Bookseller Street), named after the pseudonymous famous Yiddish author Sholem Yankev Abramovich. The Dan Hotel, built in 1953, stands tall in the background.

As the city and its population expanded north in the 1920s and '30s, small one- and two-story homes were built. Traditional Middle Eastern flat-roofed houses and European terra-cotta-tiled, sloped roofs became neighbors.

Eliezer Ben-Yehuda (1858–1922)

Moses, above the clouds of Mount Sinai, is talking on the phone with the Almighty and receiving the Ten Commandments right before the festival of Shavuot. Every holiday, this local resident takes to his wheels to deliver its particular message.

Ben-Yehuda plowed forward anyway, using several Hebrew newspapers he edited as a mouthpiece. He also helped to establish the Committee of the Hebrew Language, the organization that later became today's Academy of the Hebrew Language.

Ben-Yehuda decided to use his life and that of his family as a model, speaking to his own son, Ben-Zion, exclusively in Hebrew. Ben-Yehuda worked hard at coining words for everyday objects, such as ice cream, doll, bicycle. The collection of invented words grew with the child, proving that living in Hebrew was possible. Ben-Zion was the first person in thousands of years whose native language was Hebrew.

From the home, Ben-Yehuda's vision expanded to the nation. He began working incredibly long hours to compile a dictionary that would enable others to live in Hebrew. His seventeen-volume *A Complete Dictionary of Ancient and Modern Hebrew*, completed after his death in 1922 by his wife, Hemda, together with Ben-Zion, is an achievement of enormous magnitude, not only for Jews but for the world at large: no other ancient language was ever brought back to life like this. Ben-Yehuda was midwife, scholar, and pioneer all in one. His funeral on the Mount of Olives was attended by more than thirty thousand people who were themselves living proof of historian Cecil Roth's reflection: "Before Ben-Yehuda, Jews could speak Hebrew; after him, they did."

Ben-Yehuda Street is a long, wide street in the center of the city running parallel to the beach from Allenby to the Yarkon Park. Lined with residential buildings, its ground-floor spaces are home to an endless array of restaurants and pubs as well as high-end art galleries, jewelry stores, and Judaica shops.

ISAAC DOV BERKOWITZ STREET

ISAAC DOV BERKOWITZ WAS DESTINED to live a life of letters. Publishing his first Hebrew story, "On the Eve of Yom Kippur," at age eighteen, he went on to write many stories, novels, and plays in Yiddish and Hebrew, and translated prolifically from Yiddish and Russian into Hebrew. Born in Slutsk, Russia, to a simple working family, Berkowitz's love of literature and writing inspired him to leave his hometown for Vilna. There he became part of a new family when, in 1906, he married Ernestina Rabinovitz, the eldest daughter of the great Yiddish writer Sholem Aleichem.

Berkovitz continued to write his own Hebrew stories while beginning to translate Sholem Aleichem's from Yiddish to Hebrew. Influenced by his father-in-law, he started to write in Yiddish as well. When Sholem Aleichem decided to leave Vilna for New York, Berkowitz and his wife moved with the rest of the family. After Sholem Aleichem died in 1916,

A photo taken in Vilna, Lithuania, then part of the Russian Empire, sometime around 1904–1905. Right: Isaac Dov Berkowitz. Center: Ernestina Rabinovitz, the eldest daughter of the writer Sholem Aleichem. With them is Moshe Ben-Eliezer, a Hebrew writer, editor, and translator.

Berkowitz, as literary executor of his estate, compiled the comprehensive editions of Aleichem's work, boosting their already immense popularity.

Having his fill of yet another Diaspora, Berkowitz decided to realize his Zionist ambitions and moved to Tel Aviv in 1928. He threw himself headlong into the literary scene, editing a literary journal, *Moznayim*, adapting some Sholem Aleichem plays for Habima Theater, and writing Hebrew and Yiddish stories. Unlike other writers in British Mandate Palestine, Berkowitz did not abandon Yiddish. Out of honor to his father-in-law, and out of a deep love of the language, he remained committed to Yiddish and eastern European Jewish culture.

Yet Berkowitz is perhaps best known for his important contributions to modern Hebrew literature. Both in style and content, his fiction influenced and captured the *zeitgeist*. Hebrew had "rekindled belief in the

The official opening of the Sholem Aleichem House in 1966. Where once people came to honor the great Yiddish writer, their "Jewish Mark Twain," today stands the Tel Aviv District Court. Fiddler on the Roof was based on Sholem Aleichem's stories.

Isaac Dov Berkowitz (1885–1967)

resurrection of the dead," he said, connecting Jewish rebirth to return to both land and language. Yet his work did not idealize this return. His 1904 story, "The Uprooted," captured the alienation many young Jews struggled with. It soon became a phrase adopted by other Hebrew writers. Berkovitz's memoir, *Our Forebears as Human Beings*, is considered a work of seminal importance. It moves from the personal to the communal, while reflecting on his own life, on Sholem Aleichem's, and on eastern European Jewish communities before World War I. Berkowitz won the Bialik Prize twice and received the Israel Prize. He died in 1967 and was buried in Tel Aviv's Trumpeldor Cemetery, along with many of the country's cultural luminaries.

Berkowitz Street hugs the Golda Center, where one finds the Tel Aviv Performing Arts Center, the Beit Ariela Municipal Library, and the Tel Aviv Museum of Art. The street is a beautiful mix of 1930s and '40s residential buildings, a glass and steel modern residential tower, the Tel Aviv District Court Building, and at number 4, the Sholem Aleichem House, which opened in 1966 and hosts cultural activities and a museum space dedicated to the legacy of the great Yiddish writer.

Mothers with their babies stroll by the Museum Tower office building. Taking the lead from its neighbor – the Tel Aviv Museum of Art – the tower exhibits sculptures outside the building and paintings in the lobby.

BIALIK STREET AND CHEN BOULEVARD

Take me under your wing,
be my mother, my sister.
Take my head to your breast,
my banished prayers to your nest.

WHEN HAYIM NAHMAN BIALIK EXPRESSED the desire for Israel to return to its ancient home, he spoke not only for himself but for many of his people. Bialik's humble birth in 1873 in Radi, Ukraine, belied the title "King of the Jews," bestowed upon him by his adoring readership. One of the most beloved and famous Jews during his lifetime, he was given a 1934 funeral in Tel Aviv fit for royalty. A hundred thousand people accompanied the coffin from his house on Bialik Street to the Old Cemetery a few blocks north.

Insisting that Hebrew be brought to life, Bialik inspired an entire generation to write about modern life in the ancient tongue. He was also

Right: *Beit Ha'Ir (Town Hall) is a museum dedicated to the history of Tel Aviv. Its square fills with visitors and residents alike. Originally built as a hotel in 1924, the building was Tel Aviv's City Hall from 1925 to 1965.*

Left: *The house of the great poet Bialik is seen in the top left corner. Trees and fountains were a priority for the early city planners. While the cars might be from the 1930s, the eco-urbanism is certainly up to date.*

keenly political; from the start, his poems expressed a longing for Zion. In 1901, Bialik's first collection of poetry was published in **Warsaw, and** he was hailed as "the poet of national renaissance." This was strengthened when he wrote "City of Slaughter" in 1903 in response to the crushing Kishinev pogrom. "Your dead were vainly dead," he declared angrily in the poem. Despair and passivity were no longer acceptable responses to violence. Bialik wanted Jews to start defending themselves.

Though Bialik first visited Palestine in 1909, he remained in Odessa and ran the Dvir Publishing House. But in 1924 when Soviet authorities closed it down, the political activist and famous writer Maxim Gorky helped arrange his exit. Bialik relocated to Tel Aviv, to a house built especially for him and his wife, on Bezalel Hill Street, now renamed Bialik Street in his honor. The house's design is a blend of the Middle East and European Arts and Crafts movement, reflecting Bialik's belief that modern Hebrew culture must be rooted in the ancient past.

The "king" immediately took up the mantle of cultural and national impresario upon arrival, becoming head of the Hebrew Writers' Union, and his home and garden became a magnet for the city's artistic and political life. Meir Dizengoff, the mayor of Tel Aviv and a dear friend from Russia, was a regular visitor. When the Hebrew University in

Café Restaurant Sapir, on the southeast corner of Bialik and Allenby Streets, was one of the city's first European-style street cafés. In this 1935 photo, City Hall looks out at the burgeoning city from the street's cul-de-sac.

Jerusalem opened in 1925, Bialik delivered the inaugural address. Countrywide celebrations in honor of his sixtieth birthday in 1933 included school children who came to his home to greet him. These children already knew Bialik by name and by verse. For Bialik did not only write nationalistic poems but was famous for his love and nature poems, and his many children's songs. Translated into more than thirty languages, Bialik's poems have traveled well throughout the world.

One street could not contain the love the people of Tel Aviv felt for Bialik, so two commemorate him. The first, though quite small, is called Bialik Street, and is an urban museum rich in history, architecture, and beauty. On the corner of Allenby Street, Café Bialik occupies the spot of one of Tel Aviv's first cafés. At the cul-de-sac known as Bialik Square, residents and tourists gather around the lotus flower pool and fountain. Four museums grace this street and square: Beit Ha'Ir (dedicated to the history of Tel Aviv), Bialik House (dedicated to the life and work of the national poet), Rubin Museum (dedicated to the life and work of the painter Reuven Rubin), and the Bauhaus Foundation Museum. Eclectic and Bauhaus design reign supreme on this street of stately large homes and gardens, reflecting the aesthetic and political philosophies of the city's early designers and leaders.

The second street is an acronym of his first two names: Hayim Nahman, or Chen (the Hebrew letters *chet* and *nun*). Also small in length but wide, elegant Chen Boulevard connects two large urban complexes: Rabin Square and Habima Square. From the municipal to the artistic, this sanctuary of green reflects Bialik's life interests and stature. The boulevard boasts beautiful old trees, playgrounds, benches, bike paths, and sculptures, against a backdrop of renovated apartment buildings. Children, parents, the elderly, and a steady parade of dogs walking their people fill this boulevard day and night, embodying the best of what Tel Aviv has to offer.

Sigal Primor's elegantly placed stainless steel sculpture, Piano Pianissimo, *demonstrates the artist's interest in the relationship between art and public and private life. Look carefully and see the outlines of domesticity: a table, a drawer, a bedroom.*

As the city's population grew, construction pushed north. Chen Boulevard, built in the 1950s, continued the urban tradition of tree-lined streets and islands for pedestrians and bicycles. The residential architecture celebrated the simple, clean lines of the International Style.

Bengali Ficus tree colonnades accompany cyclists and pedestrians alike as they make their way down the stylish boulevard from Habima to Rabin Square. The Charles Bronfman Auditorium, home to the Israel Philharmonic Orchestra, elegantly blends in with the background.

CHAIM BOGRASHOV STREET

AS ONE OF THE FIRST teachers in Ottoman Palestine, and as the first principal of the Herzliya Hebrew High School established in 1904, Chaim Bograshov can undoubtedly be counted as one of the shapers of Israeli culture and society. Committed to the revival of Hebrew as the Jewish national language, he made sure all subjects were taught in Hebrew at his school. The co-ed school worked toward a secular vision of a Jewish future and had a declared mission to groom the next generation of leaders and thinkers. To this end, a dormitory was built next to the school to accommodate students from abroad who wished to study in this unique learning environment. In fact, many of the school's first classes produced prominent people who helped establish the political, social, and cultural institutions of the future country.

Bograshov himself had a traditional yeshiva education in Russia, where he was born in 1876. He thirsted for knowledge, eventually earning a PhD at the University of Bern, and returned to Russia to begin his decades-long career as a teacher. But his influence stretched beyond the classroom. Bograshov attended many Zionist Congresses both before and after he emigrated to Ottoman Palestine in 1906. He vehemently opposed the Uganda Proposal (a plan to settle the Jews in Uganda instead of in the Land of Israel) and believed that Jews would thrive only in their ancient homeland. At his school, his subject of expertise, geography, was called "Love of Homeland" and included in its curriculum field trips around the country. This learning practice is still part of Israel's educational system.

Bograshov was also not shy about holding political office and wielding political influence. For nine years he was part of the Assembly of Representatives. This elected parliamentary association functioned as the internal governing council until the first Knesset was elected in 1949. Bograshov also sat on the Tel Aviv City Council for many years. He left these positions and his beloved school in 1951 when he became a member of Knesset in Jerusalem.

The street's first private homes from the 1920s abut the unpaved road that today is a bustling four-lane, two-way street. Neighbors gather around the concrete foundations of a new home in their midst. Two of these old homes are still standing proudly until today.

Café Leon, on the corner of Bograshov and Pinsker Streets, in the early 1980s. This was a nexus for bohemian artists and musicians. A young Shlomo Gronich, one of Israel's most popular singers, enjoys the Tel Aviv sun while reading the daily newspaper.

Chaim Bograshov (1876–1963)

He died in 1963, but not before a street was named after him that bordered the neighborhood of Nordiya, which he helped establish decades earlier for poor Jews rendered homeless after riots in the southern part of the city. When he hebraized his last name to Boger, it was not known if this was a reaction to the dubious honor of having a street named after him that bordered what was basically a slum or whether he finally got around to shedding his Diaspora name, a custom among many early Zionists that Ben-Gurion himself declared was necessary.

Bograshov Street is a busy commercial street that begins at the beach and leads all the way to even busier King George Street. Filled with international food establishments – from Thai to French, Italian, and local Mediterranean – the street has cafés, fast food joints, pubs, and restaurants galore. The clothing shops are young and hip, the hairstylists prolific. Tourists and longtime residents love cruising this street.

Over 250,000 people participate in Tel Aviv's annual Pride Parade. Floats, dancers, merrymakers, and watchers fill Bograshov Street. The many cafés, bars, restaurants, and boutiques all blend in as the parade makes its way to the beach.

MEIR DIZENGOFF STREET

HE WAS KNOWN AS THE "father of the city." Meir Dizengoff not only became Tel Aviv's first mayor in 1921 but was among the early settlers on land purchased in the sands north of Yafo's ancient port in 1909, putting into motion the dream of a modern Jewish city. He was as devoted to art as he was to Zionism; the first floor of his house at 16 Rothschild Boulevard became Tel Aviv Museum's first home. After his wife Zina's death in 1930, Dizengoff donated the building to the city, and in 1948 David Ben-Gurion read out the country's Declaration of Independence from its main hall.

Born in 1861 in Bessarabia, Russia, where he received a traditional Jewish education, Dizengoff enlisted in the Russian army. After his discharge, the hardships of being a soldier inspired him to become a socialist and political activist. Arrested by the Russian authorities,

Mayor Dizengoff (left) on horseback leads the 1934 Purim Adloyada (parade of costumed people). Avraham Shapira, one of the most famous Shomrim (watchmen, the earliest Jewish self-defense movement in the country), rides with him.

Meir Dizengoff (1861–1936)

Dizengoff spent eight months in prison and there concluded that Jews could not fulfill themselves anywhere in the world but in their ancient homeland. After his release, he started the Kishinev chapter of the Zionist group Hovevei Zion (Lovers of Zion) and then went to Paris to study chemical engineering at the Sorbonne, followed by glassmaking in Lyon.

An aerial shot of Zina Dizengoff Square from the 1940s. Part of Geddes's original urban design, this iconic rotary was designed by architect Genia Averbuch. When it opened in 1938, this public space became synonymous with Tel Aviv's modernization.

Left: A small street flows out of this section of Dizengoff Street, technically Zina Square, named after the late Mayor Dizengoff's wife. This renovated Bauhaus building, now a hotel, is one of several Bauhaus structures that ring the (round) square.

View of the roundabout from the Cinema Hotel's balcony. In 2018, the circular plaza was returned to street level, and its popularity has soared. The curved Bauhaus buildings that hug the roundabout can now be seen from every point.

The first time he visited Palestine in 1892 was on Baron Edmund de Rothschild's dime. The Baron wanted Dizengoff to set up a bottle factory for his emerging wine industry. Though the venture failed, and Dizengoff returned to Odessa, the desire to live in Palestine and make a home there for himself and other Jews never left him.

When Dizengoff eventually returned to the country in 1905, he ran the Geulah Company, whose goal was to buy private land for Jews to settle on. Like Rothschild, Dizengoff understood that if the dream were to succeed, the Jewish community needed to make its own money. He opened an import-export business, and when he became mayor of Tel Aviv devoted himself to building a new seaport for the growing city that could accommodate modern commerce. In 1936, he began planning an airport outside the city as well. He loved Tel Aviv as a father loves his child and wanted to see his city develop and prosper. The people knew this about him and were used to seeing him ride through the streets on his horse. He would often stop to chat with passersby to find out how they were doing and what more he could do to make Tel Aviv better. When Dizengoff died in 1936, not only those who knew him from the city, but the entire Jewish community in Palestine came out to grieve. Tel Aviv declared an official three days of mourning.

Once called Tel Aviv's Champs-Élysées, Dizengoff Street has made a serious comeback in recent years. Dizengoff Center, the city's first shopping mall on the corner of Dizengoff and King George Street, continues to draw crowds. Zina Dizengoff Square, two streets away, has undergone a significant restoration, returning it to its original street-level roundabout with gorgeous Bauhaus buildings lining the perimeter. All along the wide road, which runs north to the Tel Aviv Port, are International Style houses, chic boutiques, and a constant stream of people shopping, chatting, and sitting in cafés watching the world pass them by.

The fountain sculpture in the center of the renovated roundabout waits for the artist Agam's coat of many colors to be reinstalled. But until then, the water dances to many different rhythms, and at night, the fountain lights up dramatically.

SHLOMO IBN GABIROL STREET

The years are a thousand
Since, broken and scattered,
We wander in exile,
Like waterfowl lost in
The depths of the desert.

THE ANDALUSIAN POET AND PHILOSOPHER Shlomo Ibn Gabirol had a hard and short life. Orphaned at a young age and suffering physical pain from a lifelong disease, he soared high in spite of it all, and his writing, including his poetry, expressed this. Born in Malaga around 1021, Ibn Gabirol had a traditional Jewish schooling. Being the time of Islamic rule in southern Spain, Ibn Gabirol threw himself into learning the Arab high culture of his time, which included literature, astronomy, geometry, and philosophy.

He wrote poems as a teenager, and it didn't take long for him to be considered one of the greatest Hebrew poets of his time, even by those put off by his haughty and biting personality. More than once, Ibn Gabirol was forced to leave one Jewish community to seek a home in another. Blending Hebrew and biblical themes with the meter and rhyme schemes of popular Arabic poetry, Ibn Gabirol influenced generations of Spanish Jewish poets after him. And though he wrote more than two hundred secular poems, it is for his religious poems, steeped

Completed in 1966, Tel Aviv City Hall is home to the mayor's office and the city council. Menachem Cohen designed it using the concrete Brutalist style favored among architects for institutional buildings in the 1950s and '60s.

A couple watches fireworks in honor of Israel's Independence Day. City Hall, designed by Amnon Alexandroni, is lit up like the country's flag, and a neon sign wishes the state and its people a very happy birthday.

Shlomo Ibn Gabirol (ca. 1021–1058?)

in Jewish texts, that he is best remembered. "Remembrance," whose poetic lines work their way through the 613 Torah commandments, is often recited in synagogues during the spring holiday of Shavuot.

On Yom Kippur, many congregations around the world recite his poem "Kingdom's Crown," considered one of the greatest poems of Hebrew literature of all time. Evoking the science of his day, the poem personifies the world celebrating its creation by God, the ultimate creator, and acknowledges the largeness out there and the smallness of the human being – who is made large again through God's grace.

Thou art One, head of all minyanim,
and in every structure's foundation
Thou art One –
and the mystery of Thy Oneness
will amaze the wise of heart,
for they know not what it is.

Metaphysics, religious devotion, and beautiful language are all rolled into one long nine-hundred-line poem.

This bird's-eye view, taken from the roof of City Hall, captures thousands of city residents in Rabin Square (designed by Avraham Yaski and eponymously renamed after Rabin's assassination in 1995) who have come to celebrate Independence Day together with music, fireworks, and good cheer.

In the 1950s, the swelling population pushed the city northward. Urban design principles were carried over from previous decades. These included wide boulevards providing air and light, populated by Bauhaus buildings with their clean lines, curved balconies, and pillars, all suitable to a modern utilitarianism.

Ibn Gabirol was also an important philosopher credited with more than twenty works written in his short lifetime. Sadly, few remain. His most significant work was ironically not attributed to him as for centuries it was preserved in a Latin translation of its Arabic original and under a Latin version of his name, Avicebron. In 1846, Salomon Munk, a German Jewish scholar of medieval Jewish literature, recognized *Fountain of Life* as Ibn Gabirol's. Written when he was twenty-eight, this work makes no mention of Jewish texts and is a Neoplatonic dialogue between a teacher and student who discuss human nature to tease out meaning and purpose and to find a rational way to support good deeds. Like all his philosophy books, *Improvement of the Qualities of the Soul* was also written in Arabic (and only later translated into Hebrew). Ibn Gabirol was only twenty-three when it was published, and it boldly set out a set of ethics that were not limited to Jewish or

From 1938 to 1980, the Tel Aviv Zoo, begun by Rabbi Dr. Mordechai Shorenstein when he arrived from Copenhagen, entertained residents of all ages. The animals found new homes in Ramat Gan's Safari Park when this urban treasure closed.

Right: *This man sings and efficiently moves with his charges on a bicycle transformed into a many-sided transport. In front, on the side, in back, and way back, he takes numerous children with him on Tel Aviv's streets and bike lanes.*

any other religious sources. Instead, he proposed that the individual was in control of his senses and so his choices.

Mostly ignored as a philosopher in his lifetime, the Malagan, as he was also known, was deeply appreciated as a poet, though he lived a lonely wanderer's life. He was a prophet without honor in his homeland, and so it is fitting that mystery surrounds his death. Neither the year nor the cause is known. All that comes down through the ages is that he died in Valencia, that he was young (in his late thirties), and that he might have been murdered.

Ibn Gabirol Street is long and wide, with two-way traffic stretching from the Yarkon River in the north to the south where it forks into Yehuda HaLevi and Carlebach Streets. Residential houses with commercial ground floors offer the best Tel Aviv has to offer: cafés, chocolatiers, bakeries, and shops of all kinds. City Hall and Yitzhak Rabin Square are situated in the middle, along with the Rabin Memorial commemorating the prime minister's tragic assassination on the street in 1995.

By the time 1970 rolled around, Ibn Gabirol had become a vibrant center of café society. Israelis love their coffee and chat. This is never more evident than on Friday mornings, when cafés are filled to capacity.

Tel Aviv has been designated as one of the most dog-friendly cities in the world. But a person's best friend can't always come to work, so a professional dog walker is essential. Dogs get their exercise and some social time in as well.

ZE'EV JABOTINSKY STREET

BORN VLADIMIR YEVNOVICH ZHABOTINSKY in Odessa, Ze'ev Jabotinsky was schooled in secular Russian schools and grew up unattached to either religion or Jewish tradition. When politics became important to him, he left school to work as a journalist. Posted in Italy and Switzerland, he published under the pen name Altalena (which means "swing" in Italian, and "Old Italian" in Yiddish) and later in life used this name for his novels as well.

Though assimilated, Jabotinsky still felt he was a member of the Jewish community and was stirred to action when his coreligionists suffered a wild rash of pogroms. He called for Jews to learn to use weapons for self-defense: "Jewish youth, learn to shoot!" His response was not entirely welcomed by those Jews who feared it might bring on an even fiercer backlash. Jabotinsky ignored these voices and organized and

Kikar Hamedina (Square of the State), designed by Brazilian architect Oscar Niemeyer, is one of the largest circular plazas in the country. The luxury residential buildings hugging its perimeter were designed by Israeli architects Israel Lothan and Abba Elchanani.

In 1964, the city was still filled with simple small stone, wood, and concrete-block plaster-clad single-dwelling structures situated on sand lots. The taller residential buildings going up to accommodate the growing city can be seen in the background.

trained Jewish militias. He insisted, "Better to have a gun and not need it than to need it and not have it."

Though Jabotinsky began to take a more active role in his people's lives and destiny, and learned Hebrew, changing his name from Vladimir to Ze'ev ("wolf" in Hebrew), he remained committed to working for the civil rights of Russia's many ethnic minorities, including of course the Jews. His inclusive vision was not limited to Russia. When he spoke of Jewish life in Palestine, he wrote, "Each one of the ethnic communities will be recognized as autonomous and equal in the eyes of the law," referring to various Muslim and Christian peoples living there.

During World War I, he and Joseph Trumpeldor formed the Zion Mule Corps, made up of Russian émigrés who fought alongside the British against the Ottomans. After the war, Jabotinsky struck out on his own, leaving mainstream Zionism, and established a new political party: Alliance of Revisionist Zionists, which included a youth wing, Betar. He

Ze'ev Jabotinsky (1880–1940)

envisioned a Jewish state on both sides of the Jordan, a state more like the nation-states of Europe, whose policies catered to the Jewish middle class, with free-market policies and a small government – a far cry from the socialist vision of the Labor Zionists.

Jabotinsky looked into the future and saw more violence and trauma. In 1936, he prepared an evacuation plan outlining the need to bring Jews from Poland, Hungary, and Romania to Palestine. In 1938, he told Europe's Jews they were living on the edge of a volcano. He continued to write, advocating emigration and armed resistance. Two years later, he was in New York raising funds for a Jewish army when he died of heart failure. He was buried there, and in 1964 his and his wife's remains were reinterred on Mount Herzl Cemetery in Jerusalem. From assimilationist to passionate nationalist, Jabotinsky became convinced that Jews had to "eliminate the Diaspora, or the Diaspora will surely eliminate you."

Running from the beach to Namir Road, with the large roundabout of upscale Kikar HaMedina in between, Jabotinsky Boulevard is one of the wide tree-filled roads that circulate light and air throughout the city streets.

Tel Aviv's café culture in all its glory. Even on a sunny winter's day, people do not give up the chance to meet a friend, have an intense conversation, and eat a delicious meal together.

ELIEZER KAPLAN STREET

ONE OF THE THIRTY-SEVEN SIGNATORIES on Israel's Declaration of Independence, Eliezer Kaplan was a builder by profession and ideology. Born in Minsk, Russia, he had a traditional Jewish education as a child and in his twenties graduated with a degree in construction engineering from the Higher School for Technology in Moscow. Both knowledge bases would be put to direct use when Kaplan moved to British Mandate Palestine in 1920. He rolled up his sleeves to work, seeing there was so much to be built – literally on and for the land, as well as organizationally.

Zionist activism came early to Kaplan. At fourteen he joined the Socialist Zionist Party and helped found the Youth of Zion movement promoting a return to Israel, farming, and collectivism. He was a member of the Zionist Central Committee and a delegate to all Zionist Congresses beginning in 1913. Most impressively, Kaplan participated in the Committee of Jewish Delegations at the 1919 Versailles Peace Conference that worked to secure rights for Jewish refugees after World War I.

When Kaplan moved to Palestine, he helped orchestrate the merger of his Youth of Zion and Young Worker movements. As a representative of this new and unified association, Kaplan participated in the Conference of the Zionist Federation in London and soon after moved to Berlin to head the association's office. Returning to Palestine in 1923, he threw himself into building, first as head of the Labor Union's Office of Public Works, later renamed Solel Boneh (Israel's first construction and civil engineering company), and later by heading Tel Aviv's engineering department and sitting on the city council.

Sarona's Community Hall, 1910. Until the 1930s, it was used by the German Templars for social and celebratory gatherings. The British Army then turned the settlement into a military camp, and the hall was used to screen movies to its troops.

These German Christian Templar buildings from 1871 have been extensively renovated, transforming one of the earliest modern European villages in Palestine into a vibrant urban location filled with cafés, restaurants, underground cellar pubs, shops, and the gourmet Sarona Market.

Eliezer Kaplan (1891–1952)

The iconic Azrieli Center defines the skyline. Completed in 1999, this trio of towers – square, circle, triangle – contains offices and a shopping mall. Moore Yaski Sivan Architects completed the original plans by Eli Attia.

When the State of Israel was established, Kaplan was elected to the Knesset as part of the Mapai Party and became both minister of finance and minister of trade and industry. He put together the country's economic policies and structured its national budgets and taxation rules.

For fifteen years, from 1933 to 1948, Kaplan was also an executive member and treasurer of the Jewish Agency. Exposure to world finance through this position helped him secure the state's first loans from Barclays Bank in London and from the United States' Import and Export Bank. It also enabled him to establish Israel Bonds. Kaplan resigned from the second Knesset because of illness. He died in Genoa, Italy, in 1952 while undergoing medical treatment. Still, his legacy lives on not only in the numerous books he published on Israel's economy, but in the institutions named after him: the Eliezer Kaplan School of Politics and Social Sciences of the Hebrew University and Kaplan Hospital in Rehovot.

Kaplan Street is a very wide and busy thoroughfare connecting Ibn Gabirol Street with the Azrieli Center, the Ayalon Highway, and HaShalom railway station. Important sites fill this street: the beautifully renovated German Templar Sarona complex with shops, cafés, and gardens, Camp Rabin (IDF headquarters since 1948), the Fiverr International building at number 8, a gorgeous restoration of the former Farmer's House, and other governmental and trade agencies.

AVRAHAM MAPU STREET

THE LOVE OF ZION, PUBLISHED in 1853 by Avraham Mapu, was the first Hebrew novel, and it was a game-changer. A favorite among Hebrew readers, the novel helped inspire the Zionist movement; its many readers wanted lives like those they read about. Set in Israel in biblical times, this was a world where Jews were farmers and shepherds, where they had political autonomy, where they walked amidst magnificent sun-drenched ancient landscapes and had romantic adventures the likes of which seemed far from the daily grind of poverty in eastern Europe. The ideal and idealized lives Mapu shared with his readers contrasted with their restricted, pained ones. *The Love of Zion* was a hit among secular Jews; it enjoyed sixteen editions and was translated into many languages, bringing the early energy of Zionism to life.

Born in Lithuania in 1808, Mapu was considered a child prodigy and eventually worked as a teacher in a government school for many years. This guaranteed income enabled him to turn his pen to writing. Years earlier, his intellectual horizons had been broadened by a chance encounter with a book of Psalms that contained a Latin translation. Mapu's imagination was fired by this other, new language, and he taught himself Latin and eventually German, Russian, and French as well. These languages opened doors for him to texts and worlds way beyond the horizons of Jewish religious society. When he decided to try his hand at fiction, he was inspired by French Romantic novels.

Mapu's writing brings together his two worlds: those of Jewish and European texts. Yet his novels also look back and forward at the same time; meaning, they take place in the ancient world, but the language is lifted from the Bible and set alongside a new modern Hebrew of his invention. This style looked to a future when Hebrew would once again be an everyday spoken language and when Jews would once more take up residence in Israel in nature's beauty and bounty, leaving the corruption of European cities and towns behind them. "Righteousness dwelt only in the forest, and faith in caves," he wrote – echoes of Hasidism,

A typical Bauhaus-inspired building of the 1930s being built at the corner of Mapu and Yarkon Streets. Being typical does not make it any less lovely. Soon gardens and trees will be planted, enhancing the built and natural atmosphere of the city.

On this street, you'll see numerous International Style buildings from the 1930s, other less architecturally significant residences from the 1950s and '60s, and ongoing construction projects with super modern apartments. Living this close to the sea is a premium.

Avraham Mapu (1808–1867)

Carved from a single tree trunk, this anachronistic wizard seems to have stepped out of a European legend – complete with long beard, long cloak, and pointed turban – to grace the front yard of this Bauhaus building and its beautifully rounded balconies.

biblical stories, and a Zionist ideal whereby the land itself would heal the nation. Up until Mapu introduced this style of writing, secular Hebrew was strictly biblical in feel, and it was the province of poetry. Mapu showed that the Hebrew language worked wonderfully in prose.

Mapu published three novels and three educational textbooks in which he outlined more modern teaching methods, particularly of Hebrew. He died in Prussia in 1867, having never visited Palestine. His powerful nature descriptions, the setting of his stories in ancient landscapes, and his dramatic twists and turns of plot, though, made the passage easier for many early Zionist activists who were determined to make the vision on his pages come alive.

Mapu Street is two blocks long. For a small and unassuming side street, it has a number of seriously splendid Bauhaus houses to its credit. With sea views on the street's western end, it is no wonder that it has become a sought-after spot for hotels and holiday rentals.

MORDECHAI NAMIR ROAD

DURING A LIFE THAT SPANNED from a humble birth in a small town in the Russian Empire to becoming mayor of Tel Aviv for nearly a decade, Mordechai Namir was to hold many governmental posts that helped shape the future not only of Israel's most cosmopolitan city, but also of the entire country.

Born Mordechai Nemirovsky in 1897, Namir had a traditional religious Jewish upbringing. As a young adult, he switched tracks and studied economics and law at Odessa University. Around this time, he also became an active Labor Zionist, attracting the attention of the Soviets. Namir was arrested in 1924, and after his release from prison, he moved to British Mandate Palestine, where he hebraized his last name.

Namir held numerous positions that led to his political career. He was secretary of Ahdut HaAvoda, precursor to the Labor Party, while directing the Statistics Department of the Histadrut (until this day the largest union, and an enormously influential institution in Israel). His energy was boundless – he became a member of Tel Aviv's city council and in 1933 joined and became a national leader in the Haganah command militia fighting against the British for Jewish independence.

Soon after the State of Israel was created, Namir served it as a diplomat posted to Bulgaria, Czechoslovakia, Romania, and Moscow. His book *A Mission in Moscow: A Honeymoon and Years of Wrath*, published in 1971, recounts the work he did there. After two years abroad, Namir returned to the Histadrut, but this time as its general secretary, though

The Ramat Aviv Hotel, serving distinguished guests from 1951 to its closing in 2005, was considered the unofficial guest house of the state. Golda Meir, who lived in the adjoining neighborhood, suggested changing the neighborhood's name to reflect that of the famous hotel, giving Ramat Aviv its name. Guests included Harry Belafonte, Danny Kaye, Eleanor Roosevelt, and the Dalai Lama.

Completed in 1958, the concrete and steel HaYarkon Bridge on Namir Street spanned the Yarkon River. It enabled vehicular traffic to reach Ramat Aviv and the northern environs, connecting the two parts of the ever-growing city.

Mordechai Namir (1897–1975)

it wasn't long before he became a Mapai Party Knesset member. For fourteen years Namir was an MK, during three of which he was also minister of labor, all the while running Amidar, a government-owned construction company responsible for building thousands of housing units for the waves of immigrants who flooded into the country in the 1950s. As if this were not enough responsibility for one man, concurrently Namir was also the mayor of Tel Aviv from 1960 to 1969. He helped accelerate the building of Tel Aviv University's campus in Ramat Aviv and created a program to clear away the impoverished neighborhoods bordering the beach. As an economist, Namir contributed to understanding Israel's history, development, and future with his books, including *Work in Progress* and *Industry in Palestine*.

Highway 2, otherwise known as the Coastal Highway, goes by the name Namir Road once it enters Tel Aviv proper. Running from the northernmost border to Shaul Hamelech Boulevard in the center of the city, the road is a major north-south artery. From residential apartment towers to a bridge over the Yarkon River, passing numerous important cultural and educational institutions in Ramat Aviv and large grassy embankments all along its most northern section, Namir Road is one of the most heavily trafficked roads in Tel Aviv.

Heading out from the transportation hub behind them, Little Red Riding Hood has nothing to fear from the Big Bad Wolf this Purim, since the man from Krypton, aka Superman, is her date for the festive carnivalesque evening.

Right: As sunset falls over the Mediterranean, this young athlete swings his way across the curved structural steel girder of the bridge connecting the north and south banks of the Yarkon River.

YEHUDA LEIB PINSKER STREET

DR. YEHUDA LEIB (LEON) PINSKER arrived at a radical and even heart-breaking diagnosis: the Jews would always be a foreign element rejected by the European body politic. He witnessed years of anti-Jewish pogroms in Russia and coined the term *Judeophobia*, an incurable, deeply irrational, almost pathological fear of the Jew. The only treatment, Pinsker claimed, was for Jews to leave the countries that preyed upon them and to create a national homeland. Born in Russia in 1821, Pinsker was among the earliest of Zionist thinkers and activists who

Café Noga closed its doors in 2015, but for decades it was a central watering hole for Tel Avivians, who loved to dance and hear the live bands that played there nightly. In the 1980s, it became a popular pool hall.

Right: A renovated Bauhaus building with a beautifully curved front corner and several rounded balconies is topped by an original grand two-story metal casement window. At street level, a lively café makes sure coffee and eats are available to the city's not-so-early risers.

Designed by Joseph Berlin in the late 1930s, Cinema Mograbi's first-floor auditorium housed Israel's early theater companies. The cinema hall was on the top floor. Its roof opened so cool air could enter in those days before air-conditioning.

In 1882, he anonymously published *"Autoemancipation!" An Appeal to His People by a Russian Jew*. Written in German, this pivotal Zionist essay called for Jews to work for political and territorial independence. He argued that Jews could not wait for others to liberate them but that they had no choice but to do it for themselves. He wrote, "to the living the Jew is a corpse, to the native a foreigner, to the homesteader a vagrant, to the proprietary a beggar, to the poor an exploiter and a millionaire, to the patriot a man without a country, for all a hated rival."

In 1884 he helped found the Hovevei Zion (Lovers of Zion) organization, which was critical to enabling the dream of return actualized by about thirty thousand Jews during the First Aliyah. Infighting between various Zionist organizations and Ottoman restrictions on immigration and land purchases made him doubt the location, but not the need for a national homeland. Pinsker died in Odessa in 1891, and his remains were reinterred on Mount Scopus in Jerusalem in 1934.

Leon Pinsker Street stretches between two famous squares: from Dizengoff in the middle of the city to Mograbi, touching corners with Allenby and Ben-Yehuda Streets. Numerous Bauhaus and Eclectic style buildings can be found along this route, some with a roster of famous tenants, including Prime Minister David Ben-Gurion and the painter Ziona Tajar. Numerous high-end residential buildings have replaced old buildings, but the iconic balconies and the proximity to the sea remain the same.

organized, wrote, and advocated this radical response to millennia of persecution.

But he did not always think this way. An earlier wave of anti-Jewish pogroms prompted him to proclaim that equal rights and assimilation were the solutions for the hated Jewish outsider. This, combined with his experience of being one of the first Jews to attend Odessa University, encouraged him to think that if only Jews became more like Christians, they would be accepted. And to some extent, he lived this vision by becoming a respected physician and director of psychiatry in a municipal hospital. But ten years of this approach came to an abrupt halt when a new wave of pogroms struck Jews throughout the Russian Empire starting in 1881. Pinsker realized that this kind of hatred had nothing to do with what Jews did or did not do. Jews were hated just for being Jews, whether they prayed and kept kosher, or whether they worked on the Sabbath and married Christian women.

SHOLEM ALEICHEM STREET

PEACE BE UPON YOU. That's what Sholem Rabinovitz, known under his pen name Sholem Aleichem, was telling readers when he started to use the pen name Sholem Aleichem in 1883. One of Yiddish's most beloved writers and humorists chose an alias to separate his folksy Yiddish writing from the "serious" literature he wrote in Hebrew and Russian. The irony of history is of course that Rabinovitz is famous for the stories and plays he wrote in Yiddish. Characters like Menachem Mendl (a modern comic hero who resists the traditional institutions and pressures of family and community) and Tevye the Dairyman (a loveable, talkative jester aware of his shortcomings and winning readers over to his side with his earthy monologues) have become hallmarks of Sholem Aleichem's work. These characters share compassion and a vision of the world as a tragically comic place where a simple, thoughtful man is still clever enough to ponder his blessings and his limitations.

Born in a small town in the Ukraine to a middle-class family, Rabinovitz had both a traditional Jewish education and a secular Russian one. At twenty years old, he began writing for Hebrew newspapers on local matters and education, and within a few years tried his hand at novels and stories in Yiddish. He spent a decade writing prolifically in Russian, Hebrew, and Yiddish. When he became the owner and editor of the Jewish People's Library in 1888, he not only gave a platform to many Yiddish writers whose work he admired, but established in the public's mind that the day of serious Yiddish literature had arrived. The project also launched Rabinovitz as an important literary critic. His devotion to education prompted him to write stories for and about children. Known as the "Holiday Stories," and published by Jewish newspapers, these tales wove themes and morals of particular holidays into everyday events.

In 1905, when Russia was hit with waves of pogroms, Rabinovitz and his family moved west through Europe and eventually to New York City. At first, he was honored as a great man of letters and was even dubbed

Left: *Builders using a concrete mixer during the construction of Dr. Felix Mintz's house at 30 Sholem Aleichem Street, c. 1926.*

Below: *In 1926, Jascha Heifetz – one of the world's greatest violinists of the twentieth century – performed at Beit Ha'am (the People's House), an important cultural and education center. About six thousand people attended this concert, whose proceeds went to institutions for musical education in the city.*

"the Jewish Mark Twain." However, this warm welcome did not last long. Rabinovitz was arrogant and unkind to other Yiddish writers, and new productions of his work did not succeed. He returned to Europe in 1907, only to come back to New York again seven years later, sick with tuberculosis. He continued to write articles and stories in Yiddish until his death in 1916. His legacy has not diminished over the years, with writings translated into dozens of languages, and the phenomenally successful Broadway musical *Fiddler on the Roof*, based on his Tevye the Dairyman stories, staged all over the world from 1964 until the present day.

Sholem Aleichem Street is a small and pretty residential street that begins near the sea. Along its short route, it meets other streets named for other Yiddish writers, such as Mendele Mocher Seforim.

One of Tel Aviv's more than four thousand Bauhaus buildings from the 1930s. Its thermometer staircase window and wooden shutters are among the beautiful details. Renovations in the White City neighborhood must follow UNESCO's strict World Heritage Site guidelines.

A dramatic emergency spiral staircase graces the back of this large Brutalist bow-shaped office building known as El Al House. Designed by Dov Carmi, Zvi Melzer, and Ram Carmi, this 1963 structure was the first multistoried office building in Israel.

HANNAH SEMER STREET

HANNAH SEMER BROKE THROUGH A considerable glass ceiling to become the First Lady of Israeli journalism. Born Hannah Haberfeld in Bratislava, Slovakia, in 1924, Semer came from a religious but modern home. While in school, she began writing for a Jewish Zionist weekly paper, *Tribuna*. This activity set her off on her life's twofold path: journalism and Zionism. When the war reached her city, Semer hid for some time. She then worked in a forced labor camp making bricks; in 1944, she was taken to the Ravensbrück concentration camp for women in Germany. When the war ended, Semer returned to Bratislava and was fortunate enough to be reunited with her mother, brother, and sister.

In 1950, Semer immigrated to Israel and soon after got her first job as a journalist, working as night editor for *Today's News*, a German-language newspaper. A year later she was hired by *Omer*, a daily newspaper written in simple Hebrew for new immigrants. This job gave her the opportunity to travel throughout the country, getting to know its many dimensions, and it also brought her into the corridors of power.

It came as no surprise that *Davar* recognized Semer's exceptional journalistic skills and brought her over from *Omer* (their supplement) to work with the big boys. At *Davar*, she was appointed parliamentary correspondent, then political correspondent, and then correspondent to the US. From reporter to editor, from radio and television host to editor in chief, Semer rose through the ranks and became the first woman in Israel to hold such a senior post. Under her leadership, from 1970 to 1990, the old-school newspaper opened itself to young journalists, to controversial opinion pieces, to a commitment to journalism above ideology, and to a satirical supplement that was soon mimicked by other papers.

A central voice in Israel, Semer remained a devoted newspaperwoman her entire life, even after retiring from *Davar*. She continued to publish essays and books, to teach journalism, and to let reporters know when

Semer with her daughter and family cat in 1970, when she became editor in chief of Davar, *one of Israel's major daily newspapers. She was the first woman to hold such a powerful editorial position in the country. It took another twenty-seven years (until 2017!) for the appointment of another woman as chief editor.*

she got wind of an important political story. She won numerous prestigious prizes and was a board member of the International Institute of Journalism. Semer published *God Doesn't Live There Anymore*, a 1995 memoir about her postwar visit to Ravensbrück. In 2003, Semer was awarded the Hadassah Women's Organization's Women of Distinction Award. And when she died two months later in 2003 in Tel Aviv, she was hailed as one of the most prominent journalists since the creation of the state.

Hannah Semer (1924–2003)

Hannah Semer Street is literally at the northeastern corner of the Bavli section of Tel Aviv. Flanked by two parks, the Yarkon River Park and a wide green rise to the east, it is a quiet residential street whose low-rise apartment buildings are typical of the neighborhood: well-kept, quiet, and hospitable.

Enormous Ficus trees help create the beautiful green canopy shading the streets near the Ayalon Highway and Yarkon Park. In this northeastern corner of the city (before the river), care was taken to create green spaces for health and recreation.

Residents of this quiet street enjoy Geddes's "green belts" (a term used to describe verdant boulevards and parks) while gazing upward at the tall buildings that bring commerce, a fast pace, and all the accoutrements of big-city life.

On my travels abroad, and especially my trips to Germany, I am very careful not to eat *treif*. It's a sort of demonstration of solidarity. But here at the doorway, at Ravensbrück, I would have eaten pork if I could have eaten at all. I would have eaten steak with cheese to take revenge on God for the deaths of my aunts and cousins, who counted the days of their *niddah* time according to the law, separated *hallah* from the dough, ran to the *dayyan* with questions about a spot on a slaughtered goose, and read from the *Ze'enah U-Re'enah* every free moment – and their reward was to be humiliated to the dust and tortured until they perished. Five minutes from Ravensbrück, I would even have eaten a baby goat cooked in its mother's milk. Instead, I took a Valium. (Hannah Semer, *God Doesn't Live Here Anymore*, 1995)

The power of the quote is compounded by the fact that Semer was a vegetarian for the last thirty years of her life.

RIVKA SIEFF STREET

"LET THE MEN GET ON with it, and we'll do the real work." So said Lady Rivka (Rebecca) Sieff, who used her considerable financial and educational privilege to better the world. Her twin passions were realized in the founding of women's organizations within the Zionist movement. Together with Vera Weizmann, she established the Women's International Zionist Organization (WIZO), an organization that until today significantly supports the lives of women and children in Israel, Europe, and the United States. Sieff remained president of WIZO for over four decades.

Born into the British Marks and Spencer retail empire, Sieff attended Manchester University at a time when it was still quite radical for women to pursue higher education. Understanding how critical education was, she made academic and vocational training for women her life's priority. She was one of three women elected to the council of the English Zionist Federation in 1918, and from her work there concluded that women needed their own organizations to focus specifically on women's issues and needs. When Sieff visited Palestine for the first time in 1919, she was distressed by the substandard living conditions of many of the young Jewish pioneers. She was especially sensitive to the particular difficulties women settlers faced. The farming economy, with its emphasis on physical strength, did not exactly encourage equal rights for women. Through WIZO, Sieff introduced various vocational programs that trained women in domestic economics (already a respectable discipline in the UK), agriculture, and other technical skills useful in a changing workforce.

After the Nazi Party came to power in Germany, Sieff organized and fundraised on behalf of Jewish refugees. Her attention was not only on those women and children who sought refuge in the UK, but on young people making their way to Palestine under the Youth Aliyah program. Her work has been acknowledged as a feat of great foresight and courage that saved thousands of lives.

Continuing work with the victims of Nazism, Sieff visited DP camps in Germany. When she testified at a special United Nations committee, she pointedly requested that the British help relieve the suffering in these camps by allowing emigration to Palestine. When the State of Israel was created in 1948, Sieff herself moved to it, while her husband, Baron Israel Moses Sieff, remained in England. WIZO, with Rivka at its head, took up many of the challenges facing the young country, from food shortages to the mass immigration of Holocaust survivors and then Jews from Arab countries. In recognition of all her philanthropic work, the Order of the British Empire was given to Sieff in 1960.

Rebecca Sieff accompanies First Lady Eleanor Roosevelt on a visit to the Hadassim Children and Youth Village. Located north of Tel Aviv, this is one of five WIZO villages in the country dedicated to giving disadvantaged youth a home and an education.

Rivka Sieff (1890–1966)

This work included, of course, the establishment of the Daniel Sieff Research Institute in Rehovot in 1934 by her and her husband (later renamed, with the Sieff family's consent, the Weizmann Institute of Science in 1949).

Rivka Sieff Street is small but not unassuming. A link between King David Boulevard and Berkowitz Street, it boasts access to the Tel Aviv Museum of Art and the Litvak Gallery's exhibitions of international glass art.

Set among a large medical center, a court building, and a prestigious arts center, the Museum Tower with its mirrored cladding captures the blue sky and flags of many countries, reflecting how high the horizons around here really are.

Wide sidewalks with a profusion of trees accommodate pedestrians and cyclists alike. This small street oasis connects the heavily trafficked David HaMelech Boulevard and the Golda Meir Cultural and Performing Arts Center with its museum, library, theater, and opera house.

HENRIETTA SZOLD STREET

WHO DOESN'T KNOW OF HADASSAH, the Women's Zionist Organization of America founded in 1912? But fewer know the story of the woman behind this legendary organization that promotes health, women's rights, education, and religious tolerance in the United States and Israel, an organization that has been, in its own words, "connecting and empowering Jewish women to effect change"? The woman behind the vision and the activism is Henrietta Szold, born in Baltimore, Maryland, to a rabbi as the eldest of eight daughters.

Szold's love of learning and literature changed her life. It inspired her to open an English-language night school for Russian Jewish immigrants and prepared her for the job of editor at the Jewish Publication Society.

Henriette Szold sits with some of the founding physicians at Hadassah Hospital, Mount Scopus. Far left: Dr. Chaim Yassky, Director General of Hadassah Hospital, who was killed in the 1948 ambush of a clearly marked medical convoy that was ferrying doctors, nurses, and medicine to Mount Scopus. Seventy-eight people were murdered that day, making it the largest loss of civilian life in Israel's history.

In addition, it motivated her to pry open the gates of the Jewish Theological Seminary, where she studied advanced Judaism, but only after promising she would not seek rabbinical ordination.

Used to being the only woman in the company of powerful men in the publishing house, in the rabbinical seminary, and on boards of various Zionist organizations, Szold knew how hard it was for a woman to succeed in a man's world, beginning with equal education. For years she had to rely on public lectures at Johns Hopkins University and Peabody Institute to expand her secular learning. Her determination to empower women is a direct result of these experiences. (Her only university degree was an honorary doctorate from Boston University that she received at age eighty-four.) Seeking a more significant role for women within rabbinic Judaism, Szold was given permission to recite Kaddish (the traditional mourner's prayer) when her mother died, since there was no son to do it.

In 1933, Szold moved to Palestine, where she felt she could make more of a difference. She, along with the Hadassah organization, supported the Youth Aliyah movement, helping thirty thousand young Jewish refugees flee Nazi Europe. At the same time, she devoted herself to social and political justice for both Jews and Arabs. Szold was a pacifist who supported the Jewish-Palestinian Peace Alliance and in 1942 helped found the Unity Party, prioritizing equality over Jewish privilege.

Szold proclaimed: "Dare to dream…and when you dream, dream big." Hadassah Hospital in Jerusalem, a world-class research hospital, is a testament to her big dreams. Its visiting nurse system, based on American models of care, was the first of its kind in the country. In 1945, she died in the hospital she helped build; she was buried on the Mount of Olives. Her words live on in the institutions and in the many lives her work and vision touched.

Henrietta Szold (1860–1945)

Situated between Arlosoroff Street and Shaul Hamelech Boulevard, Henrietta Szold Street is small and unassuming, and most of it is home to one of the best hospitals in the country, Sourasky Medical Center (also called Ichilov Hospital). This is a touching echo of Szold's profound contribution to medical excellence. A series of small lanes, filled with trees and lush garden fronts and named for five of the seven fruit species mentioned in the Bible, branch off of Szold Street, creating a village-like feeling.

Henrietta Szold addresses a graduating class of nurses in the 1930s. Nursing was only recognized as a profession in Israel in 1918. The first graduating class of twenty-two nurses completed their three-year training in 1921.

The third-largest medical complex in the country, the Tel Aviv Sourasky Medical Center (aka Ichilov Hospital) fills most of this small street. Entry to the Sourasky Rehabilitation Building and Schonbrunn Academic School of Nursing is from here.

Right off busy Arlosoroff Street, a small neighborhood piazza with a cluster of shops accommodates residents, hospital workers, and visitors. Public benches like these create a space for visits, talk, coffee, and other spirit breaks during the day.

SHAUL TCHERNICHOVSKY STREET

And I shall keep faith in the future,
Though the day be yet unseen
Surely it will come when nations
All live in blessed peace.

Then my people too will flourish
And a generation shall arise
In the land, shake off its chains
And see light in every eye.

ONE OF MODERN HEBREW'S MOST celebrated poets, Shaul Tchernichovsky often writes about the longing for peace and freedom and a new life in Palestine. Sometimes he describes King Saul or the Greek god Apollo. Sometimes there is joy found in the inspirational beauty of nature. For him, Jerusalem and Athens are not at war with each other but come together to create a new vision of Jewish life. Tchernichovsky has been recently honored by having his portrait – with his bushy mustache and head of thick curls – grace the new fifty-shekel note.

Born into a traditional Jewish family in Russia, Tchernichovsky began to show an interest in the wider world in the Russian school he started to attend at age ten. At fourteen, he relocated to Odessa, where his education was further broadened and his interest in literature and languages encouraged. It was there that he also became involved in Zionism and began writing and publishing poetry in Hebrew. But Tchernichovsky did not set out to be a poet alone. He studied medicine at the University of Heidelberg and Lausanne, and when World War I erupted, he was drafted into the Russian army as a doctor. Surviving that, he barely made ends meet in postwar Russia, eventually leaving the country to spend some years in the United States and Turkey. In 1931, when he was commissioned to write a trilingual (Latin, Hebrew, English) edition of *The Book of Medical and Scientific Terms*, he moved to British Mandate Palestine.

Tchernichovsky became the resident doctor of Tel Aviv's innovative Herzliya Hebrew High School, a role that later included other schools. In 1936, he moved to Jerusalem, where he was part of writers' organizations and the prestigious Committee of the Hebrew Language, later known as the Academy of the Hebrew Language. Tchernichovsky's

Gan Meir (named after Mayor Meir Dizengoff), which lies between King George and Tchernichovsky Streets, on the day it opened to the public in 1944. Today the park's trees are very tall, and numerous leisure and athletic sites guarantee that the park is always busy with people

Shaul Tchernichovsky (1875–1943)

exceptional abilities with language were seen in his wide-ranging translations from the English, Greek, Latin, German, and French. He wrote traditional sonnets in modern Hebrew. He wrote romantic idylls about his childhood and even lived long enough to write mournful poems about the Holocaust. Twice Tchernichovsky received the prestigious Bialik Prize for Literature.

Tchernichovsky died in Jerusalem in 1943, and over the years his reputation has not diminished. His poems have been translated into more than sixteen languages, and many have been set to popular music. "I Believe," the verse partially quoted at the head of this chapter, continues to captivate the public's interest and has even been suggested as an alternative lyric for the current national anthem.

Tchernichovsky Street is a long, narrow street that runs from Allenby to Dizengoff. Dizengoff Center punctuates its northern end, and along the way, one finds a continuous string of shops; residential buildings, many designed in Bauhaus and Eclectic styles; and some of the city's best fast food joints clustered together near Allenby.

One of Tel Aviv's hundreds of small kiosks serving fine coffee and pastries. This butkeh, *a word that means "little shack" in Hebrew, is a common-enough structure in a city where space has always been at a premium.*

Right: Ping-pong players battle it out in Meir Park. This large park contains an LGBT community center, a café, a children's playground, public gym equipment, a dog park, lawns, a fishpond, and enormous trees that provide bountiful shade and beauty.

JOSEPH TRUMPELDOR STREET

JOSEPH TRUMPELDOR WAS ABLE TO pull off a highly unusual feat in Israel: becoming a hero to both right- and left-wing political organizations. For the right, Trumpeldor represented the commitment to self-defense. Together with Zev Jabotinsky, Trumpeldor founded the Zion Mule Corps in 1915, the first all-Jewish paramilitary organization in two thousand years. As an early resident of kibbutzim, Trumpeldor represented for the left the commitment to a new socialist Jewish world order.

Born in Russia in 1880, Trumpeldor had a secular upbringing. He joined the Russian Army in 1902 and lost his left arm during the Russo-Japanese War. Rather than retire from the service, Trumpeldor insisted on remaining a soldier, saying, "but I still have another arm to give to the motherland." He returned to active duty, became a Japanese prisoner of war, and changed one motherland for another. When Trumpeldor discovered Zionism and other comrades like himself, he became committed to the cause. But first, the war had to end. When that happened, Trumpeldor received four decorations for bravery and an officer's commission, making him the first Russian Jewish soldier with so many honors.

In 1911, Trumpeldor moved to Ottoman Palestine and worked and lived in various kibbutzim until World War I forced him to find refuge in Egypt. A soldier to the core, Trumpeldor fought with British forces in the Zion Mule Corps and was again wounded, this time in the shoulder. Once that war ended, Trumpeldor returned to Palestine, now under British rule, along with many young Jews who had trained with him.

Trumpeldor died a soldier's death. In the village of Tel Hai in 1920, as a result of what some historians call a misunderstanding, Lebanese fighters battled Jewish fighters, and the outcome was grim. Eight Jews and five Lebanese were killed, Trumpeldor among them. The nearby town

Tel Hai, a Jewish agricultural settlement in the Upper Galilee, was founded in 1907. In 1920, a battle, possibly based on a misunderstanding, erupted between Lebanese Arabs and the Jews living there. Trumpeldor was among the eight Jews who were killed in the ensuing attack.

Trumpeldor Cemetery, aka the Old Cemetery, in what is now the center of the city, is a virtual Who's Who of early Zionist history. Started in 1902, it was renamed for Trumpeldor after he died in battle in 1920.

of Kiryat Shmona (Town of Eight) was named in their honor. As befits a man who became such a symbol of patriotism and military might, the circumstances surrounding Trumpeldor's death unclear.

Trumpeldor Street is perhaps most fittingly famous for the Trumpeldor Cemetery, also known as the Old Cemetery, a virtual Who's Who of Tel Aviv's political and cultural history. Running from the beach to Meir Park on Tchernichovsky Street, the mostly residential street boasts Bauhaus, Eclectic style, and many more traditional low-rise residential buildings from the 1950s and '60s. Today, upscale hotels and pubs can be found on that part of the street close to the sea, and of course, the cemetery with its old gates and high wall spans a good portion of the distance on the street's northern side.

Tel Aviv flexing its architectural stylistic arms. Architect Tzvi Harel claims the House on the Boardwalk was just a playful newspaper sketch. But local businessman Piltz loved it and built it in the mid-1990s. Since then, neighbors have sprouted beside it.

Trumpeldor Cemetery (also known as the Old Cemetery) was, in 1902, at the city's northernmost limit. The city has since grown all around it. Many of the country's early founders and outstanding artists are buried here.

CHAIM WEIZMANN STREET

THE FIRST PRESIDENT OF THE State of Israel was a man of vision. As a politician, a scientist, and an inventor, Chaim Weizmann had an enormous impact on the formation of Israel as one of the world's leading centers of scientific and technological innovation.

Born in Belarus, Weizmann came from a family of humble origins. His parents gave their children a religious and secular education, and Weizmann's aptitude for science became quickly apparent. After receiving a doctorate in organic chemistry in Geneva, Weizmann taught at the University of Geneva and then at the University of Manchester, where he was also involved in research. By the time he left the field, he held over a hundred patents, some which were of great interest to both British and American armies. As a successful scientist, Weizmann had access to influential people. He was instrumental in convincing Prime Minister Lloyd George and Arthur Balfour, England's foreign secretary, to support the idea of a Jewish state in Palestine. These discussions helped bring about the Balfour Declaration in 1917. After calling England home for thirty years, Weizmann moved to Israel in 1948. When he took up the mantle of president, he was compelled to renounce his British citizenship.

As early as his student days, Weizmann became an active and ardent Zionist. When he first visited the country in 1907, he helped establish the Palestine Land Development Company. Early on, he pushed for an institution of higher learning dedicated to science in Palestine, since he believed that science was a way to build bridges and peace. He contributed to the opening of the world-renowned Technion-Israel Institute of Technology in Haifa in 1912. Years later, in 1934, Weizmann

In this 1921 photograph, Weizmann is seen sitting with his friend and fellow scientist Albert Einstein. As president of the World Zionist Organization, Weizmann had come to the United States on a fundraising campaign. Einstein came along to help.

Weizmann at the World Zionist Conference in London, 1945, their first gathering since the start of World War II. Weizmann spoke passionately, appealing to the British government to accept Jewish statehood and to allow Jewish refugees to enter Palestine freely.

was instrumental in building another science institute, this time in Rehovot. The Daniel Sieff Research Institute, renamed the Weizmann Institute of Science in 1949, remains one of the world's leading teaching and research institutes. Weizmann was also committed to other fields of scholarship and helped found the Hebrew University in Jerusalem.

During the 1920s, he was head of the World Zionist Organization and traveled the world relentlessly selling the idea of a Jewish national homeland in Palestine to Jews and non-Jews alike. But to his fellow Jews, he said, "A state cannot be created by decree, but by the forces of a people and in the course of generations. Even if all the governments of the world gave us a country, it would only be a gift of words. But if the Jewish people will go build Palestine, the Jewish State will become a reality – a fact."

During World War II, Weizmann helped form England's Jewish Brigade, consisting of Jews from Palestine who fought with the British against the Nazis. As President of Israel, a post he held from 1949 until he died in 1952, Weizmann continued to work hard to gain support and legitimacy for the Jewish state from countries around the world. The wide street that bears his name is home to Tel Aviv Sourasky Medical Center (Ichilov), one of Israel's outstanding hospitals. The mostly residential street runs from the Yarkon Park to Shaul Hamelech Boulevard.

A Ficus tree arch at the beginning of the inlaid stone path – a characteristic entrance to a Tel Aviv apartment building. Behind it, a garden of flowering shrubs and an open-air entrance lead to a staircase and hopefully a retrofitted elevator.

Right: Part of the Weizmann City Mall, this café's outdoor seating area services the neighborhood and the Tel Aviv Sourasky Medical Center (Ichilov Hospital) adjacent to it. Indoors are a larger food court, shops galore, and an office tower.

DOWNTOWN

WITHOUT A DOUBT, THE EPICENTER of the city's downtown is Rothschild Boulevard. Wide and filled with gorgeous old trees, benches, kiosks, playgrounds, pedestrian and bike lanes, Rothschild Boulevard pulses with the energy of history and the current moment. This neighborhood's small enclave of six streets, known initially as Ahuzat Bayit, grew almost exponentially to become the Tel Aviv of today.

Amidst magnificently restored Bauhaus and International Style buildings, British Mandate and Eclectic style buildings feature in the smaller and larger streets that radiate from Rothschild's central artery. There is a feeling of intimacy here, of density, a hyper-interest in enjoying the good life and getting ahead on a world-class scale. Banking headquarters, law offices, world-famous architecture, exclusive boutique hotels, and chic restaurants serving cuisines from all over the world are close neighbors in this pocket of the city. Stroll down Sheinkin Street, home to a bohemian chic scene. Bustle with the crowds on Allenby and Herzl Street, the older commercial strips of the city. Shop for the freshest fruits and vegetables in the Carmel Market. While Tel Aviv might not be known for its illustrious synagogues, at 110 Allenby Street, one can find the exception to the rule. The Great Synagogue, built in 1926 with an enormous dome and stained glass windows, was styled after European synagogues that would later be destroyed in the devastation of World War II. It is a well-known downtown landmark.

On nearby Ahad Ha'am Street, the Shalom Tower (built in 1965) still stands tall and proud: its thirty-four floors made it the first skyscraper in the Middle East.

The area known as "downtown" is filled with a vibrant mixture of architectural styles, many beautifully exemplifying their individual and outstanding elements. This beautifully restored 1926 Eclectic style building, with its blend of eastern and western flavors, stands at the corner of Montefiore and Karl Netter Streets. While cars and bicycles fill these urban streets, the copious trees and gardens bring beauty to residents and passersby.

AHAD HA'AM STREET

THE CHARISMATIC ASHER ZVI HIRSCH GINSBERG, who took the pen name Ahad Ha'am – a phrase from Genesis 26:10 meaning "one of the people" – believed that Jews needed a cultural and spiritual revival. He believed that only by reconnecting to their ethnic roots, which included reinstituting Hebrew as their daily language, would Jews be able to stem the tide of assimilation and strengthen themselves in the face of anti-Semitism. A prominent leader of the movement of cultural Zionism, Ahad Ha'am claimed that Herzl's political Zionism, the dream of a literal return to the land, was not practical. He predicted its failure and great despair, as in other times of false messiahs. He also insisted that a society of Jews not based on traditional Jewish values was unto itself a failure. "A Jewish state and not merely a state of Jews" was the goal, he claimed.

Born in Ukraine in 1856, Ahad Ha'am had a traditional Jewish upbringing. He rejected the rigidity of Jewish law but remained devoted to Jewish ethics and culture. He looked forward to Jews returning to the ancient homeland, but not in masses. He foresaw a strong core of individuals creating a spiritual and cultural center that would revive Jewish ethics and fortify embattled Jewish communities around the world. These communities would then support the growing community in Israel.

Starting in 1891, Ahad Ha'am made many trips to Ottoman-ruled Palestine. After his first trip, he published an essay, "A Truth from Eretz Yisrael," in which he condemned political Zionism for distorting the facts on the ground: the land was not empty; farming land was hard to purchase; young settlers faced many hardships. In another essay years later, he critiqued these same young Jews for treating local Arabs disrespectfully. He claimed they were acting against traditional Jewish values and cited Proverbs 30:22, which warns against slaves becoming kings. Those Jewish settlers who allowed their new sense of power to warp their ethical judgment were acting totally contrary to the purpose of

In the early 1910s, one-story and two-story structures marked a growing urbanization on one of the oldest streets in Tel Aviv. The addition of roads, sidewalks, and street lamps was no small thing for a municipality in its infancy.

As the city increased in population, so did commerce. This photograph from the 1930s or '40s shows people window-shopping in the many ground-floor commercial establishments, an architectural element that would be repeated throughout the city.

Ahad Ha'am (1856–1927)

Tzedek. Filled with beautiful and newly renovated Bauhaus and Eclectic style buildings, it also features more modern structures, including the home of the Tel Aviv Stock Exchange and many residential houses.

Tsiporen House, built in 1925, named after the family who bought and saved it from demolition in 1985. Classical shapes – wrap-around balconies, arches, and floor-to-ceiling windows – reflect the desire to bring together ancient and modern Mediterranean cultures.

returning to the land. Instead of building a spiritual base, he said, they were entirely invested in political power plays.

Eventually, Ahad Ha'am's priorities – Jewish culture and spiritual life – were also adopted by the larger Zionist platform. Hebrew was seen as an integral part and traditional Jewish values as a springboard for the new society. In 1908, Ahad Ha'am moved to London, where he worked for the Wissotzky Tea Company and helped negotiate the language of the Balfour Declaration. Eventually, he relocated to Tel Aviv in 1922, becoming a member of the executive committee of the city council until 1926. He died in 1927 and was buried in the Trumpeldor Cemetery.

Starting at Habima Square, lengthy Ahad Ha'am Street runs parallel to Rothschild Boulevard all the way past Allenby Street and into Neve

On one of the oldest streets of Tel Aviv, this Eclectic style building, sporting Grecian style decorative columns and balcony railings, wooden shutters, and sea gray plaster, has been recently renovated and restored to its original beauty.

WHEN THE BRITISH ARMY, UNDER the direction of General Edmund Allenby, defeated the Ottoman Empire and captured Jerusalem on December 9, 1917, Jews around the world were mesmerized. For as it turned out, this was also the first day of Chanukah, the Jewish holiday celebrating the defeat of Greek forces in Jerusalem more than two thousand years earlier. Though Allenby may not have been aware of the holiday, he was fully aware of the holiness of the city. He dismounted from his horse and, together with his men, walked modestly on foot through Jaffa Gate. Then he addressed the people from David's Tower:

Since your City is regarded with affection by the adherents of three of the great religions of mankind, and its soil has been consecrated by the prayers and pilgrimages of multitudes of devout people of these three religions for many centuries, therefore do I make it known to you that every sacred building, monument, holy spot, shrine, traditional site, endowment, pious bequest, or customary place of prayer, of whatsoever form of the three religions, will be maintained and protected according to the existing customs and beliefs of those to whose faiths they are sacred.

Before this historic moment, Allenby, nicknamed "the Bloody Bull," had already made a reputation for himself fighting in the Second Boer War in South Africa. At first, he was not sure why his government wanted to open a fighting front in the east when the world war on the western front was so critical. But he did as commanded and went on to become the major hero of Britain's Middle Eastern campaign. Under his command, British troops defeated Ottoman forces in Egypt, Sinai, Gaza, Palestine, and Syria. General Edmund Allenby shaped the face of the Middle East as we know it today. When he visited his troops on the front lines, he won their respect. When he used air power and agreed to finance irregular forces from the local population working with T. E. Lawrence (aka Lawrence of Arabia), he showed vision.

The legendary Café Sapir on the corner of Allenby and Bialik Streets was one of the city's first European-style street cafés. Seen here with its large rounded façade, it was enormously popular, filling up even its rooftop seating.

At the end of the war, British Mandate rule was established, and Allenby became high commissioner for Egypt and Sudan from 1919 until 1925. For all these achievements, he was made Viscount Allenby of Megiddo and of Felixstowe in the County of Suffolk. Considered one of the first modern generals, Allenby had come a long way from rather modest beginnings in Nottinghamshire, England, where he was born in 1861. He was an active traveler and speaker after retirement, and thus it was quite a surprise when he died suddenly from a brain aneurysm in 1936. He was honored by having his ashes buried in Westminster Abbey.

Edmund Allenby (1861–1936)

Allenby Street is one of the most bustling commercial strips of Tel Aviv. Beginning at Herbert Samuel Street by the sea and stretching all the way south to Ha'Aliyah, it has offices, banks, shops without end, cafés, pubs, and more buses than you can count. Sixty percent of its buildings have been designated as historical landmarks. Running into Allenby are two more major shopping streets: the bustling Carmel Market and Nachlat Benyamin, a center for textiles that also hosts an outdoor arts and crafts fair twice a week.

In the 1920s, Allenby Street was a busy thoroughfare for camels carrying sand and crushed seashells (zifzif), the major substance used for construction of the city. The Venetian-styled building that now sits at the corner of Allenby and Yonah HaNavi Street, built in 1922, is today covered by a nondescript façade, masking the beauty of the original building.

Café life is always abuzz on crowded Allenby Street. The paneled mirror façade reflects activities across the wide, busy street where the intersections of King George Street and fashionable Sheinkin Street are on view.

A typical morning at the mouth of two markets: the Carmel Market with its abundance of fresh produce, shops with prepared foods and other sundries, and cafés and bars; and the crafts market featuring artists from all over the country.

ARTHUR BALFOUR STREET

ARTHUR JAMES BALFOUR, 1ST EARL of Balfour, is perhaps most remembered for the letter he wrote as British foreign secretary on November 2, 1917, to Baron Walter Rothschild, an important leader of England's Jewish community. He asked Rothschild to pass the letter on to the Zionist Federation of Great Britain and Ireland. In it he wrote:

> I have much pleasure in conveying to you, on behalf of His Majesty's Government, the following declaration of sympathy with Jewish Zionist aspirations which has been submitted to, and approved by, the Cabinet.

> "His Majesty's government view with favour the establishment in Palestine of a national home for the Jewish people, and will use their best endeavours to facilitate the achievement of this object, it being clearly understood that nothing shall be done which may prejudice the civil and religious rights of existing non-Jewish communities in Palestine, or the rights and political status enjoyed by Jews in any other country."

This letter, which became known as the Balfour Declaration, set the political environment for an increase in immigration of persecuted Jews from Russia and other eastern European countries to British Mandate Palestine. Friends with Chaim Weizmann since 1905 and sensitive to the Jews' suffering, Balfour wanted to offer them an alternative place to live. But he was also adamant that this other place not be England and supported strict anti-immigrant legislation aimed at closing the doors to these very same Jews. Balfour was often called the Second Cyrus, for like the ancient Persian king, he too made a declaration that the gates of the Jewish return to their ancient homeland needed to be opened.

Born in East Lothian, Scotland, in 1848, Balfour came from an aristocratic and political family. He went on to have a long and distinguished career in politics as a member and leader of the Conservative Party.

Two lords share a moment. Lord Alfred Balfour, wearing chaps and holding a riding crop, chats with Lord Walter Rothschild. Balfour's November 1917 letter to Rothschild made public England's intention to support the creation of a Jewish homeland in Palestine.

Children play in the new street going up near their homes, whose design shows a mixture of elements: white and colored plaster, stone façades, arched windows, and wrought-iron balcony railings. The trees – the finishing touch – would come later.

Arthur Balfour (1848–1930)

He served as secretary for Scotland (1886), chief secretary for Ireland (1887–1891), prime minister of the United Kingdom (1902–1905), first lord of the Admiralty (1915–1916), and foreign secretary (1916–1920). In addition to all this political activity, he was also a devoted thinker and academic. His book *Defence of Philosophic Doubt*, published in 1879, in which he makes the claim that human reason alone cannot define truth, established his reputation as a serious thinker. It hints at the road not taken: he chose to devote his professional life to politics rather than lead a quieter, more contemplative life in the academic ivory tower.

For over fifty years, Balfour served in the British government. In 1922 he was made Earl of Balfour and Viscount Thaprain of Whittingehame and thereafter sat in the House of Lords. His 1930 funeral was a private affair as he requested and is consistent with the man whose aloofness prompted the creation of the new adjective *Balfourian*, meaning reserved, detached, inherently superior, and smug.

Balfour Street is a small street in the heart of Tel Aviv. Running through Rothschild Boulevard to Yehuda HaLevi Street at one end and Allenby Street on the other, this street boasts some of the most beautiful Bauhaus and Eclectic style residential buildings in the White City.

This beautiful Eclectic building has not only been gracefully renovated, but has received a multistory addition set back from the street to not take away from the lovely period details: arched windows, wooden shutters, stone railings, ribbed columns.

Eager to hand out a pair of candles to female passersby so they will light them and welcome in the Sabbath that evening. The table set for four, including wine goblet and silver candlesticks, whets the spiritual appetite.

YISRAEL BARZILAI STREET

THE ZIONIST MOVEMENT WAS NOT exempt from conflicting visions of its ultimate goals. Theodor Herzl's political Zionism believed the Jewish people needed a practical solution – a homeland of their own to free themselves from relentless persecution. Asher Ginsberg, aka Ahad Ha'am, had a different vision. His spiritual Zionism contended that the Jewish people first needed a spiritual renaissance so that when they returned to their ancient homeland, they would become a "light unto the nations," not merely another people seeking to realize national aspirations.

Yisrael Barzilai was a writer who reached the same conclusion as Ahad Ha'am and devoted his life to spiritual Zionism. Raised in a rabbinical family, Barzilai was born Yehoshua Eisenstadt near Minsk, then part of the Russian Empire. Active in the Hibbat Zion movement, he immigrated to Ottoman Palestine in 1887 but was disillusioned with the physical and psychological hardships, the poverty, the battles with disease, and mostly with the Jewish community's lack of commitment to a spiritual life.

Barzilai returned to Russia and became a founder of B'nei Moshe, a clandestine movement led by Ahad Ha'am dedicated to developing spiritual Zionism. Simultaneously he was on the Executive Committee of the established and powerful Hovevei Zion movement in Odessa and worked openly to promote immigration to the new Jewish settlements. Still, he wrote numerous articles, among them "The Wrong Way" and "Way of Life," describing the harsh realities waiting for Jews who moved to Palestine without preparing themselves spiritually. He believed that their task as Zionists was not just to pick up and move, but "to broaden the scope of nationalism, elevating it to an ethical ideal based on the love of Israel, and embracing moral values."

Sharon Garden, created in 1925 by the Department of Urban Tree Planting, was the city's second public park. Its four and a half acres provided a place for leisure and sport, a green respite in the city.

But Barzilai didn't stay away for very long, and in 1890 he returned to Israel. In addition to documenting the First Aliyah's hardships in articles and stories, he also helped establish schools and libraries in Yafo and Jerusalem – institutions that nourished the spirit. He was openly against the Uganda Proposal (a 1903 offer wherein a portion of British East Africa would be given to the Jewish people as a homeland). For spiritual Zionists, a Jewish homeland on any other land but Israel would be a travesty of home. He was openly against the influence of Baron de Rothschild on the young communities and was among the early wave of writers and thinkers who promoted both Jerusalem and Hebrew as central features of a Jewish return.

Barzilai was a prolific writer, and in 1912 a collection of his shorter works was published. But soon afterwards, he was forced to leave the country during World War I and never returned. In 1918, he died of illness in Switzerland. Out of respect for his life's work, in 1933 his bones were reburied on the Mount of Olives.

Yisrael Barzilai Street in the Gan HaChashmal (Electricity Park) neighborhood downtown is only three blocks long but filled with shops, pubs, cafés, and a great deal of surprising and thought-provoking street art. The Sharon Garden in the middle of this mix is an oasis of trees, benches, and wooden paths.

A handsomely restored Eclectic style building with hints of British Mandate in the Gan HaHashmal neighborhood (Electric Park neighborhood) named for the city's first power plant. Like the bougainvillea here, the park offers a green respite from plaster and concrete.

Right: *A Bauhaus building with curved balconies and a glass-block staircase wall waits for a loving renovation. Meantime, neighborhood residents can feast their senses on the delights of this ground-floor plant nursery and even take home a plant or two.*

THEODOR HERZL STREET

THE FOUNDER OF POLITICAL ZIONISM, Theodor Herzl wrote in his 1902 novel *Old-New Land*, "If you will it, it is no dream." This line became the Zionist movement's call to action. Born Binyamin Ze'ev Herzl in Budapest, Herzl grew up in a well-off, secular family in which his grandfather talked about a Jewish return to Israel. Though he studied law at the University of Vienna, his passion was literature. He wrote poetry and plays, and he also worked as a journalist; Herzl's life was radically altered covering the 1894 Dreyfus trial in Paris. The governmental anti-Semitism on display, the crowds calling for Dreyfus's death as a traitor and as a Jew forced Herzl to question assimilation as the solution for European Jewry. In 1896 Herzl published his book *The State of the Jews*, in which he outlined his vision of political Zionism. This led to a storm of controversy throughout the Jewish world. Those already involved in Zionism embraced Herzl. In London, a mass rally was held, and he was publicly given responsibility for leading the

movement. Other Jewish communities in Europe quickly followed suit and recognized Herzl as their leader. But other Jews condemned him, feeling threatened by the radical idea of returning to the ancient homeland, whether because this secular vision was not divinely sanctioned or because they remained committed to assimilation. But Herzl was undeterred, firmly believing that "no nation can be redeemed save by itself."

From that time on, Herzl devoted himself to the cause. He organized congresses and met political leaders, including German emperor Wilhelm II, Ottoman sultan Adbul Hamid II, and Pope Pius X, looking to them for support for the vision of Jewish return. In his 1902 novel *Old-New Land*, Herzl drew a literary portrait of life in the homeland. His was a multicultural vision of a country where many languages would be spoken, where all would have equal rights regardless of religion, and where a free-market economy would be balanced by generous

In 1909, the Herzliya Hebrew Gymnasium, the country's first Hebrew high school, moved from Yafo to Herzl Street. This beautiful façade, designed by Boris Schatz (founder of the Bezalel School of Art), was the major landmark of Tel Aviv. Unfortunately, in 1959 this beautiful landmark building was torn down to make way for the Shalom Tower.

A color-tinted postcard of Herzl Street from the 1920s. Contrary to the tranquil promenade shown here, it is today a bustling commercial street. The original architectural splendor of this part of Herzl Street has remained largely preserved.

Theodor Herzl (1860–1904)

social programs. For Herzl, Zionism meant tolerance and justice for all peoples.

But dying young at the age of forty-four did not allow him to see his vision realized. Although he died in Vienna in 1904, in 1949, Herzl's remains were moved to Mount Herzl in Jerusalem, to what would become the country's national cemetery for dignitaries and fallen soldiers.

Like a river that meanders through the city, Herzl Street is long, action-packed, and intersects with many important streets. Beginning at Shalom Tower, it reaches south into Yafo and the Russian Church at number 157. Herzl Street boasts a whole host of building styles, old and new, neglected and restored. Tel Aviv's first shopping arcade, the Pensak Passage at number 16, opened there in 1925, and Herzl Street remains a prominent commercial center until today.

The Meir Shalom Tower, Israel's first skyscraper, completed in 1965 was for a time the tallest building in the Middle East. Yitzhak Pearlstein, Gideon Ziv, and Meir Levy were the architects. The legendary Herzliya Gymnasium was torn down to accommodate this development zeal.

WHEN SIR MOSES HAIM MONTEFIORE entered a room, he commanded attention. At 190 centimeters (6'3") tall, he was a powerful figure who carried with him not only great wealth but vision. In his time, he was the most famous British Jew. Born to a Sephardic Italian mercantile family that moved to England generations earlier, Montefiore was born in Leghorn (Livorno), Italy, during one of his father's extended business trips. Back in London, he was raised as a proud Jew, well aware of the political and economic restrictions on his people's progress and liberties. Even still, he increased his family's wealth significantly when he became one of twelve Jewish stockbrokers allowed in London, personally handling his finances and those of Nathan Mayer Rothschild, the brother-in-law of his wife, Judith Cohen. With high intelligence and the kind of foresight he would later apply to the destiny of the Jewish people, Montefiore became one of the wealthiest men in England.

Children play on one of the most beautiful streets in the city, then and now. The Eclectic style building on the right, known as the Pagoda House, was built in 1924. Its rounded balconies are decorated with appliqués and flower boxes.

A Jewish New Year greeting card shows off Montefiore Street. A cluster of residents and passersby face the camera. Not far behind them the street ends. But not for long. Development and construction continued apace.

It is said that Montefiore spent the first half of his life making a fortune and the second half spending it on philanthropic causes. His first of seven trips to Ottoman-ruled Palestine in 1827 changed his life. Not only was his religious observance strengthened and his commitment to helping the impoverished Jewish communities there emboldened, but his imagination was ignited. He saw in the Holy Land the answer to Jewish persecution and wrote in his diary that he would "form a company for the cultivation of the land and the encouragement of our brethren in Europe to return to Palestine.... By degrees I hope to induce the return of thousands of our brethren to the Land of Israel. I am sure they would be happy in the enjoyment of the observance of our holy religion, in a manner which is impossible in Europe." At the same time, he donated large sums of money to promote education, industry, and health among Palestine's Jewish community.

Sir Moses Haim Montefiore (1784–1885)

Pagoda House, a 1924 Eclectic building designed by architect Alexander Levy, is a local icon. The city's first residential elevator was installed to accommodate the Polish ambassador who resided on the third floor. The building was restored in the 1990s.

Montefiore died in 1885 just shy of his 101st birthday. A few months earlier, his hundredth birthday was celebrated all over the world.

Montefiore Street boasts some of the most beautiful architecture in Tel Aviv. Located in the heart of the city, it features many finely restored buildings from the 1920s and '30s that exemplify Bauhaus and Eclectic styles and are now home to quality boutique hotels, chic restaurants, and trendy pubs.

To alleviate the terrible overcrowding and squalor inside Jerusalem's Jewish Quarter, in 1855 Montefiore, as executor, used funds from the estate of American philanthropist Judah Touro to buy land outside the Old City walls. Today this neighborhood, Yemin Moshe, is one of the most beautiful in Jerusalem. The original buildings have become part of the cultural center and artist guesthouse, Mishkenot She'ananim. The neighborhood's windmill built by Montefiore in 1857 so that Jews could grind their own flour remains a visual testament to his efforts toward Jewish self-sufficiency.

Montefiore also worked relentlessly to improve the plight of European Jews. He traveled to Russia, Italy, Romania, and Syria to plead the Jewish cause. In all places, he was treated respectfully by political and religious leaders, as befits the once sheriff of London, a man knighted by Queen Victoria, who was later elevated to the rank of baron. Sir Moses

This beautiful 1926 Eclectic style building designed by architect Dov Tchudnowski was restored in two phases ten years apart, by two different owners. Its eastern and western elements boast ornamental balcony railings, columned cornices, arched windows, and fluted decorative columns.

ROTHSCHILD BOULEVARD

WHEN BARON EDMOND JAMES DE ROTHSCHILD first visited Ottoman Palestine in 1889, he was inspired. He saw that the "renaissance of Israel and of that ideal so dear to us all, the sacred goal of the return of Israel to its ancestral homeland," as he wrote later to the pioneers, had suddenly become a vision that could be realized. "The Famous Benefactor" and "Father of the Yishuv," as he came to be called, was born in 1845, a member of the French branch of the Rothschild family. The baron though was not interested in banking. Art, science, and philanthropy were his passions. Together with his brother, Alphonse, they helped create the French Committee, providing aid for Jewish refugees fleeing Russia. He shared the vision with these refugees and reduced his art acquisitions to buy land in Palestine. Baron Edmond de Rothschild helped establish more than thirty communities in the Jewish Yishuv.

Today's fine wine industry can thank the Baron and his vision. He brought over French experts to help plant vineyards in Rishon LeZion

A view of Rothschild Boulevard's western end in the late 1920s. In the distance on the right-hand side is Hotel Ginosar (which still stands today). At the end of the mall is the electrical transformer, which provided power for that part of the city's buildings and street lamps.

In 1910, the launch of Rothschild Boulevard included the city's first kiosk and streetlamp, located on the corner of Herzl Street. The boulevard also underwent a name change: from Rehov Ha'am (Street of the People) to Rothschild Boulevard.

Tall Ficus and royal poinciana trees line large portions of the boulevard's median island. A tremendous source of beauty and shade, the trees invite residents and visitors to stroll, ride, and take a seat on one of the boulevard's many benches.

Baron Edmond Benjamin James de Rothschild (1845–1934)

A view of Rothschild Boulevard years into its development, in 1911. The boulevard of today is easily recognized in this early rendering, despite the empty lots, mostly one-story homes, and newly planted saplings seen here.

In 1934, at the age of eighty-nine, Baron Edmond James de Rothschild died in France. Twenty years later, he and his wife were reinterred in the Ramat HaNadiv Memorial Gardens located between Zichron Ya'akov (named in memory of his father) and Benyamina (named after the baron himself). But death did not stop his philanthropy. Funds to build the Knesset in Jerusalem were donated in his memory by James Rothschild, his son. And the communities and factories, wine industry and educational institutions the baron helped establish continue until today,

and Zichron Ya'akov. He established farming schools in which Hebrew was also taught and said he looked forward to hearing poems in modern Hebrew. The baron's generosity extended to health clinics, swamp draining, factories that produced agricultural products, flour mills in Haifa, and even a silk factory in Rosh Pina. His ability to see into the future led to the construction of an electric station in Naharayim. And his respect for the past caused him to sponsor archeological digs, most notably in Jerusalem's City of David.

Rothschild was a great humanist who spoke about the need for cooperation between Arab and Jewish communities. He wrote to the League of Nations that "the struggle to put an end to the Wandering Jew, could not have as its result, the creation of the Wandering Arab." Involved in the passing of the Balfour Declaration, Rothschild was elected honorary president of the Jewish Agency at its formation in 1929.

A contemporary street party surrounds Mayor Dizengoff, who sits proudly on his horse in front of Independence Hall at number 16. Originally Dizengoff's home, this was where Ben-Gurion read aloud Israel's Declaration of Independence in 1948.

providing livelihoods, garnering awards, and realizing the dream of Jewish renewal day after day.

It is so very apt that Rothschild Boulevard is one of the most dynamic streets in Tel Aviv. Its wide promenade filled with sculptures and children's playgrounds is an island of calm and fun for pedestrians as cars race by on either side. It is set against a dazzling backdrop of Bauhaus and other old residential buildings. If its beautiful old tall trees, reams of benches, bike lanes, playgrounds, small gardens, and tranquil pools with bulrushes were not enough of a draw, the small cafés that serve excellent coffee and little sandwiches on nearly every corner of the promenade cement the invitation welcoming residents and visitors alike.

Rothschild Boulevard's popularity is not new. Designed as the city's first public space in 1910, it was always a great people-watching spot. The town planners hoped to build a boulevard that would match the splendor of any found in Paris. So after the sycamore trees were planted for shade and beauty and the benches strategically placed beneath them, the city's first kiosk selling newspapers, orange juice, and soda was built

Dozens of acro-yoga pairs show off their balancing skills in front of Habima Theater. This enormously popular public space, aka Habima Square, boasts cultural institutions, gardens, and an eternity pool. It is the termination point for grand Rothschild Boulevard.

Located at number 46, the Levine House, designed by Yehuda Magidovitch in 1924, is an Eclectic style building known for the pointy tower on the roof. In later decades it housed the USSR embassy, and even later Sotheby's auction house.

The Edmond de Rothschild Center at number 104 is an art and cultural center dedicated to innovative Israeli art and research. This Bauhaus-inspired Expressionist building was designed by Judah Stempler and built in 1928.

The 1940s housing stock that went up on the eastern edge of Rothschild Boulevard, seen here at the corner of Marmorek Street. Directly across from Habima Theater, these White City buildings, designed by the architect Yehoshua Steinbuk, celebrate the utilitarian Bauhaus vocabulary with modest rounded balconies and white plaster exteriors.

on the corner with Allenby Street. And the public was invited to come to see and be seen. And they did.

Initially called Rehov Ha'am, Street of the People, the boulevard was renamed in 1910 because residents wanted to honor Baron de Rothschild for his many contributions to the community. Later many Bauhaus and International Style buildings were built along the boulevard, including Dizengoff House at number 16 (now Independence Hall), where in 1948 David Ben-Gurion read aloud Israel's Declaration of Independence.

As befits a financial and cultural center, the boulevard boasts numerous art galleries and museums, such as the Haganah Museum at number 23, Sommer Gallery for Contemporary Art at 13, and Alon Segev Gallery at number 6. The Edmond de Rothschild Center at number 104 is a lovely example of an Eclectic Expressionist building, and the 1934 Bauhaus Krieger House at number 71 has been beautifully restored. Rising alongside these older buildings are glass and steel towers designed by great contemporary architects, such as I. M. Pei and Richard Meiers.

MENACHEM SHEINKIN STREET

IN 1910 WHEN THE EARLY group of Jewish settlers set about building new homes and lives in the land they had bought north of Yafo, they needed to come up with a name for their new community. Menachem Sheinkin, as one of the neighborhood founders, suggested they call it Tel Aviv, after the recent Hebrew translation of Herzl's novel *Altneuland* (*Old-New Land*). Not only did it seem to be an appropriate manifestation of the vision of Jewish settlement in their ancient homeland, but Tel Aviv had, as the ever-pragmatic Sheinkin pointed out, "a local, Arab sound and so the local population will be able to get used to it quickly." The building committee liked his idea, and his proposal was adopted.

Born in Russia in 1871, Sheinkin was orphaned at an early age and was sent to live with a well-established family who provided him with a traditional Jewish upbringing and education. Interested in languages and politics, he studied philology at the University of Odessa and became active in the Zionist movement. To understand the challenges faced by young people in Ottoman Palestine, he visited the country before attending the Zionist Congress in 1900. And a few years later, in 1906, he moved to Yafo, where he set up the Odessa Committee's Immigration Office and directed the World Zionist Organization office.

Unlike many of his peers, Sheinkin was not enamored of socialism. He thought it too narrow an agenda, which would prevent young Jews from immigrating. Jews were comfortable in cities, and while some would happily make their way to socialist farms, the majority would only feel at home if they could practice their professional skills within an urban environment. Sheinkin believed that these Jews should be appreciated just as much as the "mythic" farmers were. He was not eager to accept into the country the many thousands of poor families fleeing Russia and used his position in the Immigration Office to encourage them to move to America instead. He was marginally successful.

The large central intersection of Sheinkin, Allenby, King George, and Nahalat Binyamin Streets and the Carmel Market was called the Star of David Square. Bauhaus principles are architectural vocabulary for the building on the left. The building on the right is Eclectic style all the way.

Clothing and jewelry boutiques, cafés, and plenty more trendy shops line Sheinkin Street. Passersby are lured by the ripe-banana hairdo of a mannequin perched on a motorbike to stop and seek the refreshment of a freshly squeezed fruit juice combo.

Menachem Sheinkin (1871–1924)

Committed to education and advancement, Sheinkin was one of the founders of the Herzliya Gymnasium in Tel Aviv and was instrumental in securing land in Jerusalem for the Hebrew University. For a few years during World War I, Sheinkin was forced to leave the country. He spent those years in America but returned to Palestine again, this time under British rule, in 1919. He resumed his political work and, on another trip to America in 1924, was tragically killed in a car accident in Chicago. He returned home in a coffin and was buried in Trumpeldor Cemetery.

Following his death, Sheinkin was honored by having a street named after him near Allenby, devoted to tailoring, jewelry making, and other crafts. In recent decades, this street has become one of the most fashionable and fun streets in the city. Running from Allenby to Rothschild, Sheinkin Street remains one of the best people-watching streets in town. Come ready for the tempting fashions and cafés as well.

At one of the most heavily trafficked intersections in the city, pedestrians cross three streets in one go -- Sheinkin, King George, and Allenby – on their way to the Carmel Market.

YITZHAK SADEH STREET

NICKNAMED "THE OLD MAN" WHEN he was the commander of the elite Palmach fighting force before Israel's War of Independence, Yitzhak Sadeh might have been "old" in years and military experience, yet was "young" enough in energy and vision that he provided the emerging country with the tools it needed to protect itself. By instituting various types of fighting units and strategies, Sadeh left a solid imprint on the development of the unique Israel Defense Forces.

Born Yitzhak Landoberg in Russia, Sadeh had a traditional Jewish upbringing and education yet joined the Russian army during World War I. Like Joseph Trumpeldor – whom he met in 1917 – Sadeh was decorated for bravery for his role in battle. These two courageous war veterans used their military experience for the benefit of the Land of Israel. Together they envisioned a much-needed Jewish defense force, and when Sadeh moved to the country in 1920, he immediately set to work.

In the next three decades, Sadeh was to become one of the most important military leaders and strategists in the country. Among his contributions was the establishment of mobile patrol units, the special commando unit of the Haganah, the introduction of armored brigades, and the founding of the Palmach (the basis of future elite IDF units). In 1945, he left his position as commander of the Palmach to become chief of general staff of the larger Haganah organization. In this role, he oversaw the military struggle against British occupying forces. At the same time, he was committed to using his fighting forces' intelligence and abilities to smuggle Jews who had survived the Holocaust into the country. His poem "My Sister on the Beach," published in 1945, uses the symbol of a young woman who survived the worst of Europe as the rallying cry for the fight for Jewish independence. Elsewhere, Sadeh used the Maccabees as a symbol for his soldiers "fighting without fear – for faith, the right to faith, for the homeland, to live free in the homeland, self-defense, to stand in battle and in the end, victory.

And their blood, let's say it in all simplicity and confidence, flows in our veins. We are exactly like them."

As a member of Hapoel (the worker) sports association, he was an avid advocate of sports and physical education in the country. When Israel achieved its independence, Sadeh, aged fifty-nine, retired from the army and moved to Yafo. As a civilian, he devoted himself to writing

The Maariv Intersection was named after Maariv, the Hebrew-language daily newspaper, whose building, designed by Yaakov Ben-Sira (and demolished in 2019), and logo are seen on the left. This was and remains a busy intersection, as can be seen in this 1962 photo.

Yitzhak Sadeh (1890–1952)

In 1966, the country's first Cinerama was built. Over the years, it also was used as a discotheque. Its round structure was known far and wide, which didn't stop it from being closed and demolished in 2016.

stories, plays, and nonfiction about his childhood and about the young heroes who died for the sake of an independent country of their own. He often used the pen name The Wanderer. Sadeh died in Tel Aviv in 1952 and is buried in Kibbutz Givat Brenner.

Yitzhak Sadeh Street starts at the busy Maariv Intersection and runs east crossing the Ayalon Highway until it reaches Moshe Dayan Street. A wide, multilane thoroughfare, this street is characterized by its modern office buildings, its older residential housing, and many traffic lanes.

This mixed-use residential and commercial tower under construction joins others that already exist and is one of many others that will go up in the future. The Hassan Arafa neighborhood alongside the Ayalon Highway is transforming into a vibrant hub.

BEACH

FLYING INTO ISRAEL, ONE CANNOT help but see and admire the Mediterranean Sea and the way the city hugs it from one end to the other. Tel Aviv is, above all, a beach city. Large and small hotels line the seaside streets of HaYarkon, Herbert Samuel, and Kaufmann. The newly renovated promenade, the Tayelet, with its shaded seating areas, its stone benches stepping down to the beach, its curves and rises, invites residents and visitors alike to walk, run, bike, stroll, sit, and relax beside the Mediterranean. All along the streets that run parallel and perpendicular to the sea, strong breezes fill the air with the clean smell of salt air. From any spot, on the sand, on a bench, from one of the many new hotels and residential buildings that face the water, the blue sea beckons, and amazing sunsets invite calm and awe.

Tel Aviv is a beach city, and individual beaches – from the religious beach to the gay beach, from the drummer's beach to the dog beach – offer the full gamut of water sports. No matter your interests, you can find people swimming, windsurfing, board and body surfing, sailing, kayaking, stand-up paddle boarding, and just sunning. In the sand, people do calisthenics, yoga, stretching; they are busy in the municipal all-weather outdoor exercise gyms. And when exercise is not on the agenda, one has an ample choice of cafés whose tables, chairs, and sun umbrellas are on the beach itself, making it possible to enjoy a cold coffee while digging one's toes into the cool sand and watching the waves move in and out.

On land and on the sea, Tel Aviv's beaches are a paradise for sea-goers and sun-worshippers alike. Twelve months a year you'll find people enjoying the beauty of Israel's Mediterranean coastline.

DAVID FRISHMAN STREET

IN THE LAND OF ISRAEL, a 1913 travelogue by David Frishman, describes his impressions from two earlier visits to the country in 1911 and 1912. These were significant trips because Frishman had not always been a Zionist. Born in Poland in 1859 to a well-off, religiously observant family, but one that was also sympathetic to the Jewish Enlightenment movement, Frishman felt very much at home in Europe. And like many Europeans, his allegiance was to the culture and history of the continent. The idea of leaving it all behind to move to the Middle East, where so much was unknown and "uncultivated," was not especially appealing to him.

Something of a prodigy, he began writing and publishing in Yiddish as a teenager. Devoted to this language, he sought to stretch Yiddish into a wider European canvas and introduced some of the elements of early Modernism and Romanticism into his work. Yet he was suspicious of adapting Hebrew to contemporary life and did not think Hebrew could or even should be made modern. He thought the literature being written and published in Hebrew was mediocre and openly criticized Eliezer Ben-Yehuda for his work on a modern Hebrew dictionary. But all this changed as he began to read Bialik and other gifted writers. The challenge, he then said, was to make sure to write Hebrew well. Frishman said art came before ideology and that the quality of writing was more important than any nationalistic content.

He too began to write essays and stories in Hebrew and edited books and journals that promoted the work of some of the best modern Hebrew-language writers. Frishman translated European classics into Hebrew and was highly respected for his essays. Only after he visited Palestine did he realize that Hebrew and Jews had a future there. He wrote: "Today, anti-Semites in Poland are angry because they are still mired in the world of long ago, whereas Jews have moved on and become modern and are no longer willing to put up with this sort of thing." Swept up by the landscape, the budding farming communities, and the urban centers all using Hebrew as their everyday language, Frishman continued to advocate for excellence in Hebrew literature. After a few months in a German prison during WWI as a foreign national, he

Café life has always been essential to Tel Avivians, as seen in this 1964 photo outside the now-defunct Café California and the original entrance to the Cameri Theater.

David Frishman (1859–1922)

The 1930s Hod Workers' Residence, designed by Arieh Sharon, was an expression of the country's political, social, and economic agenda. This communal residence had a kindergarten, reading rooms, a general store, doctor's clinic, and social spaces for residents to gather.

returned to Russia, where he lived, wrote, edited, and published many important works in Hebrew, until his death in 1922.

At the corner of Frishman Street and the beach is the Dan Hotel, the first luxury hotel in the city. All along the street are beautiful, impressive buildings and institutions. Of the many Bauhaus and International Style buildings located here, one of the most fascinating is the Hod workers' cooperative housing unit at number 35, designed as an urban commune with apartments built around an interior garden.

Virtual gridlock as pedestrians and vehicles make their way down to the sea to see the Israel Air Force's Independence Day Flyover. This annual favorite draws out the crowds, both on land and on sea.

This juice seller literally wears his wares, drawing attention to his fabulous fruits and juice combinations. His little shop also offers customers coffees, teas, and other beverages, as well as brochures with information about the health properties of nature's candy: fruit.

HERBERT SAMUEL PROMENADE

IN 1902, AT THE AGE of thirty-two, Herbert Louis Samuel was elected to the British Parliament. He was the first Jew to hold a cabinet position; those who came before him had converted to Christianity. A member of the Liberal Party, Samuel was an avid supporter of social reforms, including women's right to vote. Born in Liverpool in 1870, Samuel studied at Oxford University, where he moved away from Judaism and religious belief in general. Yet his brand of atheism did not stop him from keeping kosher and the Sabbath.

As early as 1915, Samuel advocated a British protectorate in Palestine, helping create the context for the Balfour Declaration (support for the establishment of a Jewish homeland in Palestine). When Samuel was appointed high commissioner of Palestine in 1920, he would become the first Jew to rule over the land since Herod came to power when Israel fell to the Romans two thousand years earlier. Also in 1920, Samuel was appointed Knight Grand Cross of the Order of the British Empire. It was especially significant that he recognized Hebrew as one of the three official languages in Mandate Palestine, English and Arabic being the other two. It is also important to note that he tried to mediate between the Jewish vision of return and Arab resistance to Jewish immigration. Caught between a rock and a hard place, he was not able to please either side. Yes, he helped usher in the Balfour Declaration, but at the same time he slowed down Jewish immigration into Palestine to help keep the peace. For Jews, these restrictions were a slap in the face. For Arabs, Samuel represented a colonial regime, and any degree of Jewish immigration supported the uprooting literally and politically of the local Arab population.

Samuel was high commissioner for five years and then returned to Britain to become the leader of the Liberal Party from 1931 to 1935. In 1937 he was titled Viscount Samuel of Mount Carmel, and much to the dismay of Jews around the world, he supported Neville Chamberlain's appeasement policy toward Germany. One year later, he became an important supporter of the Kindertransport, a project that spirited Jewish children out of Germany and Austria and into the United Kingdom. Their lives were saved because they spent the war years living with host families. In 1941, he again became the leader of the Liberal Party. He held this position until 1955. When the new medium of television became something to be reckoned with, politicians understood its power. At eighty-one years of age, Samuel was the first British politician to deliver a speech on TV, reaching into thousands of homes.

The Herbert Samuel Promenade is a long and windy street that hugs the shoreline from Gordon Street in the north to the Neve Tzedek

A 1970s photo of Atarim Square, designed by Yaakov Rechter and Werner Joseph Wittkower, under construction. The intention was to create a hub of social activity between beach and boulevard. After a few good years, the square went into decline.

Herbert Samuel (1870–1963)

Bicycles and scooters traverse the length of the beach in designated lanes bordered by tall, elegant palm trees. Riding by the sea with the wind and salt air is a pleasure on any day, but particularly on sunny winter ones.

neighborhood in the south. Cars move down its many lanes. On one side of the wide street, cyclists and pedestrians luxuriate in the beautifully renovated boardwalk. On the other side, a mass of hotels, embassies, and cafés beckon passersby.

Cars have multiple lanes to move southward along the beach. The Dan Hotel, the first hotel built on the beach, became even more of a landmark in the 1970s when Yaakov Agam installed his rainbow mosaic on the western façade.

This wide bird's-eye view of a swath of the Tel Aviv beach shows in lovely detail how the water meets the sand, the sand meets the promenade, and the promenade meets the street and city grid.

NOT ALL JEWS TURNED THEIR backs on their early religious upbringings when they became active in the Zionist movement. Some, like Yehezkel Kaufmann, looked to find a balance between ancient traditions and modern developments. As one of the great Bible scholars of the twentieth century, Kaufmann examined the history of the Jewish people – as a religion and as a nation – and published many admired works of scholarship on the subject.

Born in the Ukraine in 1889, Kaufmann received an outstanding Jewish education. After exhibiting great talent in his primary schooling, he studied with two progressive religious teachers: Rabbi Chaim Tchernowitz in Odessa and Baron David Günzburg in Saint Petersburg. From there, his interests widened. He enrolled in the University of Bern, Switzerland, where he deepened his knowledge of traditional Jewish texts but also included the study of Western philosophy. In 1918, he received a doctorate in these respective fields.

When Kaufmann moved to British Mandate Palestine in 1928, he settled in Haifa, where he taught at the private Re'ali School. He researched and wrote continuously, and for these efforts, in 1933, he received the Bialik Prize for Jewish thought – the first time this prize was ever awarded. He remained in Haifa until 1949, when he moved to Jerusalem to become a professor of Bible studies at Hebrew University.

Kaufmann's contribution to the field of biblical studies is noteworthy. His four-volume work *Exile and Estrangement: A Socio-Historical Study on the Issue of the Fate of the Nation of Israel from Ancient Times until the Present*, published in 1930, looks at Jewish history from a sociological perspective. He concluded that it was Judaism as a religion – its laws, rituals, and learning – that preserved the Jewish people as a nation throughout its tumultuous history. While this book was received with great respect, it also upset many scholars. For Kaufmann was also noting that secular Zionism could not be the answer to Jewish destiny.

Over the next thirty years, Kaufmann would bring out eight volumes of his most important and famous work, *The Religion of Israel: From Its Beginnings to the Babylonian Exile*. In it, he analyzes the history of Judaism and its literature and claims that the "Israelite religion was an original creation of the people of Israel. It was absolutely different from anything

This 1960s photo clearly shows the demolition of the Manshiya neighborhood, established by Yafo Arabs one hundred years earlier. The 1914 Hassan Beq Mosque and the partially demolished building housing the Irgun Museum are the only original structures remaining today.

Yehezkel Kaufmann (1889–1963)

the pagan world knew; its monotheistic worldview has no antecedents in paganism." This view was considered quite radical and received considerable attention. Kaufmann received the Bialik Prize again in 1956 and the Israel Prize in Jewish Studies in 1958. He died in Jerusalem in 1963.

Yehezkel Kaufmann Street hugs the Mediterranean Sea from the Neve Tzedek neighborhood in the north to the start of Yafo in the south. One side of the wide multilane thoroughfare buzzes with the din of pedestrians, bikes, and cars. On the other, modern hotels line the street.

One-story private homes in the Neve Shalom neighborhood show the contrast between the older buildings and their newer replacements. In the background and in stark contrast, we see multistory, high-end office buildings on Kaufmann Street.

The beach is a magnet for all. This religious couple is making good use of an air walker in one of the sport stations that are free and open to the public every mile or so along the beach.

An aerial shot going south toward Yafo. The 1916 Ottoman style Hassan Bek Mosque, whose minaret was reconstructed in the 1980s to twice its original height, is set before a bevy of large modern-style hotels.

SHLOMO LAHAT PROMENADE

"THE CITY THAT NEVER STOPS!" That's how Shlomo "Chich" Lahat envisioned Tel Aviv. And that is what the city became under his successful four-term governance. Lahat, the city's eighth mayor (1974–1993), transformed Tel Aviv from the small cultural hub of the country to a world-class metropolis featuring the arts, entertainment, beach culture, finance, and cuisine attracting tourists from all over the globe.

Born Shlomo Lindner in Germany, Chich moved to British Mandate Palestine in 1933 with his family. After attending the prestigious Gymnasia Herzliya high school in Tel Aviv, he joined the Haganah and fought in the War of Independence. Later in the Israel Defense Forces, Chich honed his leadership skills as governor of East Jerusalem after the June 1967 war and commander of operations at the Suez Canal during the 1967–1970 War of Attrition. By the time Lahat retired from the IDF, he held the rank of major general.

Chich understood that to grow his city and make it exceptional, he would have to invest in its physical, educational, and cultural infrastructure. Which he did. The list of his accomplishments is astounding. From opening places of entertainment on Saturday so city residents could access them on their weekend to rehabilitating the beaches and the sea, Chich prioritized the community's needs and wishes. Lahat also understood the value of the thousands of Bauhaus buildings in Tel Aviv and established a select committee to oversee the preservation and restoration of these architectural gems.

President Reuven Rivlin called Chich the Herod of Tel Aviv, referencing the ancient king's spectacular building projects, some of which, such as Masada and Caesarea, are still with us today. The Lahat Promenade, which he built (and which was renamed after him in 1998), made the beachfront not only aesthetic and clean, but also accessible. Residents

A 1980 photo of Atarim Square, showing its early popularity. The location was inviting, its concrete mushrooms and round forms iconic. Eventually, the design by Yaakov Rechter and Werner Joseph Wittkower was considered flawed, and the public turned away from the multilevel plaza.

A 1986 aerial shot of the Gordon Pool, built in 1956, famous for its saltwater and Olympic-length lanes. Adjacent to it is the Tel Aviv Marina, the first in Israel, built in the 1970s.

and visitors alike are invited to stroll, run, bike, and relax on a bench facing the beautiful sea. Among the outstanding cultural projects and buildings Lahat helped realize were the Suzanne Dellal Center for Dance and Theater, the Tel Aviv Cinematheque, the Israeli Opera, and the Gesher Theater.

After his tenure as mayor, Chich did not retire but held numerous prestigious positions, including chairman of the Museum of the Jewish People (Beit Hatfutsot), president of the Council for Peace and Security, chairman of Yad Vashem Fund, and member of the board of governors of Tel Aviv University. As a tribute to his enormous contribution to the city, Lahat was buried in Trumpeldor Cemetery, joining the city's historical elite.

Over four kilometers long, Lahat Promenade begins at the Tel Aviv Marina and runs south alongside the beach to the start of Yafo. In recent years, it has been renovated, expanding on Chich's original 1980s design.

Amphitheater-like steps lead down to the beach. Not only do they provide easy and seamless access to the beach, the steps themselves have become a destination. Visitors chat, lounge, read, and relax here with friends, children, and pets.

MAX SIMON NORDAU BOULEVARD

MAX SIMON NORDAU IS PERHAPS best known for two contributions to Jewish history. The first is cofounding the World Zionist Organization with Theodor Herzl in 1897. The second is his advocacy of athleticism and the body beautiful among Jews.

Born Simon Maximilian Südfeld in 1849 in Hungary, Nordau was a thoroughly assimilated Jew who turned his back on Orthodoxy. He changed his name, moved to Paris, married a Protestant woman, and said, "Since then I have always felt as a German and as a German only." Judaism had become "a mere memory." All this was to change during the 1894 Dreyfus Affair. Like many other early Zionist leaders, Nordau felt that the unjust and flagrantly anti-Semitic prosecution of Dreyfus proved that Jews in the Diaspora would always be persecuted.

At the First Zionist Congress in Basel, Switzerland, which he helped organize, Nordau, the physician-psychiatrist, spoke passionately of

The Bauhaus, utilitarian buildings that served as workers' homes of this most northern neighborhood, many designed by Arieh Sharon, are surrounded by open spaces and gardens. In this photo from 1943, two women take a group of children for a walk on the stone paths.

On Tu b'Shevat in 1936, children plant the trees that today line this broad boulevard and that have grown to provide us the much sought-after shade today.

Max Simon Nordau (1849–1923)

Clearly marked bicycle lanes provide a safe environment for the many people who share the wide median island: those on foot and those on all sorts of wheeled devices. The island starts at the beach and reaches Ibn Gabirol Street.

Mother and daughter are a real-life parallel to the blue and white pedestrian traffic sign a little way behind them on the boulevard. Should we tell them they are on the wrong side of the dividing line?

"muscular Judaism," about the need for Jewish bodies to come out of closed rooms into the bright light of day to relearn skills and strength, to become farmers and warriors again. The long Diaspora had weakened the Jews, he claimed, and in their homeland, they would integrate mind, body, and spirit. He especially revered Bar Kochba and saw him as "a hero who refused to suffer any defeat. When victory was denied him, he knew how to die. Bar Kochba was the last embodiment in world history of a battle-hardened and militant Jewry."

At the Sixth Zionist Congress, Nordau supported another provocative position – the settlement of Jews in Uganda. Since Palestine's Ottoman rulers were not cooperative, he and Herzl believed another solution to Jewish vulnerability in Europe was needed. This unpopular position almost cost him his life.

Nordau's extremist views were not limited to the Jewish world. In a number of his books, most famously *Degeneration*, published in 1892, Nordau denounced European art and society as decadent and nihilistic, and by the turn of the twentieth century, his work had been translated into more than eighteen languages.

Nordau Boulevard in the city's Old North neighborhood is the last wide boulevard before the Yarkon River and its park. A wide pedestrian island filled with tall palm trees, bike lanes, benches, and kiosks, it provides green relief and opportunities to stroll and roll from Ibn Gabirol Street to the beach. Built in the 1950s and '60s, the houses on the boulevard are simple three- and four-story buildings with lovely gardens in front and balconies above that enable residents to enjoy the strong sea breezes that wind their way down the wide street.

SOUTH, NEVE TZEDEK, FLORENTIN

THE CITY'S SOUTHERN NEIGHBORHOODS SUFFERED decades of decline and neglect. In recent decades this has turned around. Neve Tzedek, built in 1887, began a slow gentrification in the 1980s, and in the late 1990s, the same trend started in Florentin, a neighborhood developed in the 1920s and named for David Florentin, a Greek Jew who bought the land for his beleaguered community. Though both neighborhoods have experienced renovation, the differences between them are distinct and make for a fascinating urban fabric.

Neve Tzedek is filled with old small homes, alleyways, and new residential projects that, for the most part, try to maintain the original ambiance of the quarter. Its streets are filled with chic boutiques, restaurants, galleries, and the lovingly refurbished Suzanne Dellal Center for Dance and Theater, home to the internationally renowned Batsheva Dance Company and dedicated to showcasing other acclaimed Israeli and foreign dance companies.

Florentin was and remains a working-class industrial neighborhood. Its revitalization was inspired not by the well-to-do, but by artists drawn to the large industrial lofts and rock-bottom rents. While signs of gentrification are everywhere, Florentin retains its charming grittiness and industrial cityscape. With a reputation for being one of the hippest neighborhoods in the world, Florentin is famous for its street art, its pubs and clubs in seemingly abandoned basements and lofts, its cafés filled with artists, and not least for the Levinsky Market, robust with ethnic foods and spice shops.

Both gritty Florentin and artsy Neve Tzedek are welcoming, colorful examples of a city in transformation – on an upswing – rediscovering and reinventing itself.

The façade of this house on Chelouche Street features an artist's playful take on the denizens of Tel Aviv.

AHARON CHELOUCHE STREET

UNINTENTIONALLY, AHARON CHELOUCHE HELPED CREATE the future city of Tel Aviv. Out of love for the land, he used his considerable wealth to buy acres of dunes north of Yafo. And out of love for the land, he dedicated himself to promoting coexistence between the Arab inhabitants and the many Jews who had already begun to arrive.

Chelouche was born in Algeria in 1840 and, as a small child, moved to Ottoman Palestine with his parents. The family eventually settled in Yafo, where Chelouche received a traditional Jewish education. He learned to be a gold- and silversmith, as well as a moneychanger. A brilliant and talented young man, he became wealthy and a significant figure in the Jewish community.

In 1887, tired of Yafo's crowded conditions, Chelouche bought land to the northeast of the city and decided to build a large house for his family. At the time, this was no-man's-land, and it took some persuading to get his family to agree to move. Chelouche House, at 32 Chelouche Street, was the start of today's charming Neve Tzedek neighborhood. Though this was the first Jewish settlement outside of Yafo, Chelouche did not intend to create a new Jewish city or even neighborhood. It did not take long, however, for other Jews, including Chelouche's son, Yosef Eliyahu, to realize that more land was needed to accommodate the growing number of Jews pouring into the country from Europe. But even before Yosef Eliyahu became one of the founders of the city of Tel Aviv, his father bought land even further north and sold it to a community of Yemenite Jews in 1904. That neighborhood, known as the Yemenite Vineyard, remains a lively place today, filled with small homes, restaurants, and old-world alleyways. Chelouche bought hundreds more acres of land outside of Yafo that eventually became the newer neighborhoods of Neve Shalom and Ohel Moshe.

Chelouche prided himself on being an Arab Jew. He spoke Arabic fluently, wore a caftan and fez, and successfully navigated Yafo's channels

Directly in front of the electric wires lies the wadi housing the remains of the late-nineteenth-century train tracks, once connecting Yafo to Jerusalem (closed in 1948). In the coming years, the new light rail will once again pass through this neighborhood.

Aharon Chelouche built his very large house at number 32 in 1892. Built primarily as a residence for his family, it also housed a synagogue on its eastern side, and the Tachkemoni Religious School for boys, founded by HaRav Kook in Yafo.

Aharon Chelouche (1840–1920)

of culture and commerce. This bicultural identity helped grease the wheels of his real estate dealings and the construction supply business he and his sons developed, providing iron, tiles, and cement to contractors. Until he died, Chelouche promoted coexistence and business as forces of the future. When he died in 1920, he was buried among Tel Aviv's important personalities in Trumpeldor Cemetery.

Chelouche House at number 32 is an important Tel Aviv landmark slated for conservation. Once isolated among sand dunes, today it is at the center of the bustling artistic and picturesque neighborhood of Neve Tzedek. Starting one block from the sea and running south to Eilat Street, Chelouche Street is filled with small red tile-roofed buildings and new residences that maintain the area's charm. Number 42, one of the first in the city to have electric lighting, continues to shine light as Neve Schechter – Legacy Heritage Center for Jewish Culture. Its diverse cultural and religious programs draw in people from many backgrounds.

Ceramic sculptures and tiles decorate an already beautiful entrance to an art gallery at number 16. The red metal door and decorative floral appliques stand out dramatically inside the stone doorframe's Grecian-inspired jambs, head, and pediment.

Beit Tamar (Tamar's House) built in 1929. The date appears in Hebrew letters in the corner piece below the roof. Artist Tamar Shalit-Avni renovated the building and playfully decorated the walls and cornice with her ceramic figurines.

ELHANAN LEIB LEVINSKY STREET

LIKE MANY EARLY ZIONIST WRITERS and activists, Elhanan Leib Levinsky was raised in a traditionally Jewish household. Born in Lithuania, he had a Talmudic education and was encouraged to read the Jewish Enlightenment literature, which is how he came across author and scholar Moshe Leib Lilienblum. This was a turning point, since it not only inspired him to become a writer himself but also to challenge the rabbis, as had Lilienblum.

At eighteen, Levinsky published his first articles and abandoned his medical studies to become involved in the Hovevei Zion and the BILU movements promoting Jewish emigration to Palestine. After visiting Palestine in 1882, he returned to Odessa to continue to write and promote Zionism. For a while, he worked for Carmel Wines selling wines made in Palestine.

As a writer and Zionist, Levinsky was so passionate about Hebrew as the language of the Jewish future that he spent years criticizing Yiddish literary greats such as Sholem Aleichem. Eventually, he came around and accepted that both were languages that Jews could and would write in excellently, and he wrote in both for the rest of his life. *Voyage to the Land of Israel in the Year 2040*, written in Hebrew and published in 1892, was his futuristic utopian novel, which took the form of a travelogue in

A woman and two children stand in the middle of a developing Levinsky Street in the 1930s. Trees were planted as homes were built to ensure that nature remained part of the growing urban environment.

Aharon Eitin was the pioneer of the Tel Aviv printing industry. Eitin House at number 69 is a grand building in the Eclectic style, designed by Alexander Levy. It features rounded, extruding windows with a brass cupola and a tall, arched main entrance.

Elhanan Leib Levinsky (1857–1910)

One of the many markets selling nuts and dried fruit street side. Inside the shop, coffee, teas, honey, tehina, fruit concentrates, and condiments are ready to be bought and brought into the kitchens of the city to enliven meals.

People line up to purchase burekas from a neighborhood shop. Baked savory phyllo dough pastries filled with potato, cheese, spinach, or mushrooms, burekas are originally from Anatolia and the Balkans. They are one of the more popular foods in Israel.

the Jewish State of Israel. It is an idealized portrait in which justice, workers' rights, and a technologically progressive government prevail. He wrote, "In the past, our forefathers traveled to Jerusalem by way of Paris, and because they found themselves in Paris, forsook continuing to Jerusalem. Now the order is turned. We travel to Paris by way of Jerusalem, and when we come to Jerusalem, we forsake Paris. How times have changed!" Visions of an idealized future society were a not uncommon staple for early Zionist writers. One has only to think of Herzl's *Altneuland*, published ten years later in 1902, to be reminded of this.

Levinsky is most famous for his Hebrew-language cultural column called "Thoughts and Deeds" in which Rabi Karov, the narrator character, talks intimately to readers about cultural and political issues with humor and insight. Until his death in 1910, Levinsky was at the center of Odessa's Jewish literary, political, and educational circles. His funeral was attended by tens of thousands of people who came to pay their respects to a man who with great warmth and openness brought humor and the vision of Zionism into their lives.

Levinsky Street is best known for the gourmet market that runs down both sides of the narrow road. Started by Salonika Jews in the 1930s, specializing in and catering to Balkan cuisine, the market soon expanded to include Jews from Iran as well as immigrants from other countries. This is the place in the city to buy spices, herbs, smoked fish, herring, nuts, dried fruits, teas, coffee, baked goods, and foods from many cultures. Alongside the market stalls today, and branching out into the many side streets, one can find some of the city's trendiest cafés, pubs, and restaurants, all of which buy their food fresh from Levinsky Market.

MOSHE LEIB LILIENBLUM STREET

BORN IN 1843 IN LITHUANIA, Moshe Leib Lilienblum went through two significant changes in life that mirrored developments seen throughout the Jewish communities of eastern Europe. Being a writer and an activist, he influenced thousands among his Yiddish-reading public. The first concerned religion; the good Jewish boy who learned, studied, and even founded a yeshiva then became a voice for radical reform. In his writing, Lilienblum demanded a "closer connection between religion and life" and asked rabbis to reinterpret laws so people's lives would be made easier. During a famine in Lithuania, he pleaded that the rabbis use leniency and allow the hungry to eat legumes during Passover. But instead of seeing the kindness and the logic in his words, they denounced Lilienblum as a radical free thinker and banished him.

The violence and riots that swept through southwestern Imperial Russia from 1880 to 1884 brought on Lilienblum's second awakening. Jews were blamed for the assassination of Czar Alexander II, resulting in mass bloodshed. Lilienblum, like Herzl in France, recognized that the Jewish minority in Europe would always be vulnerable to anti-Semitism and that Jewish emigration to Eretz Yisrael was the only solution. When the Hovevei Zion organization was founded in 1884, Lilienblum became its secretary, a position he held for the rest of his life.

Through his articles, poems, a play (the first Hebrew-language theater piece performed in the Yishuv), two autobiographies, and other scholarly works, he helped the Jewish community become familiar with the Zionist commitment of return to the ancient homeland. And when he died in Odessa in 1910, he was considered one of the most influential writers of the early Zionist movement. Lilienblum enthusiastically believed in modernity and change. He advocated an undoing of the Jewish people's very long exile. Only then, when Jews were politically and economically autonomous and not living under the fist of a

This photo from the 1910s shows (left to right) the Eden Cinema (Tel Aviv's first cinema and now only a shell of a building), the first of the two Chelouche "twins" houses, and Lilienblum 3, some of the first stone and plaster houses of the new Ahuzat Bayit neighborhood, or as it was later renamed, Tel Aviv.

This color-tinted postcard from 1927 shows the swift progress over the years as more houses and urban amenities became part of the street's landscape. On the right, with its green turret roof, is the telegraph and post office.

Moshe Leib Lilienblum (1843–1910)

government that hated them, would they be able to heal and thrive, in body, mind, and spirit.

One block south of Rothschild Boulevard, small Lilienblum Street was one of the first six streets in Tel Aviv. Some of the city's most trendy restaurants and bars can be found here, located in a familiar architectural mix of Bauhaus, Eclectic, and British Mandate style, along with contemporary glass and steel buildings. Lilienblum Street is the place to wine and dine. When Lilienblum said, "There is no remedy for a man who starts looking upon life with unrelieved pessimism," he could not have known how the street named for him would come to reflect the exact opposite energy. Optimism and a zest for life are felt in every footfall of this street. When Eden Cinema, Tel Aviv's first movie house, opened at number 4 in 1914, it too was an expression of this man with a vision for the future. While the cinema building needs renovation and attention, it is a concrete trace of Lilienblum's confidence of the Jew living differently – as a cultured world citizen – in the ancient-young home.

At number 14, this Eclectic style building was part of Ahuzat Bayit, Tel Aviv's first neighborhood. Rudi Weissenstein lived here. He was a photographer well known for documenting life in Israel in the early and middle decades of the twentieth century.

This little blue kiosk at number 3 is one of the few that remain from the 1920s. Once serving patrons of the defunct Eden Cinema across the street, it has a new lease on life since its beautiful restoration.

SHALOM SHABAZI STREET

If there be no mercy left in the world,
The doors of heaven will never be barred.
The Creator reigns supreme and is higher
than the angels.
All, in His spirit, will rise.

KNOWN AS THE SHAKESPEARE OF Yemen, Rabbi Shalom ben Yosef Shabazi wrote poetry that expressed the pain, sorrow, and hope of Yemenite's long-suffering Jewish community. The rise of the Zaydī dynasty in 1629 brought with it many persecutions. Then in 1679, by decree of King Imām al-Mahdi Ahmad, the Jews were exiled to the desolate region of Mawza. Shabazi was among the displaced, and he captured the trauma of this event in his poem "Tidings Have Reached Us." He was known as Rabbi Shalom Shabazi, and his *diwan* (collection of spiritual poems) was received as morale-uplifting lessons for the embattled Jewish community. Out of the more than fifteen thousand he wrote, only about 850 of his poems are known today.

Born in the town of al-Sa'id in 1619, Shabazi prided himself on a lineage that hailed back to Judah, the fourth son of the patriarch Jacob. Shabazi had a traditional Jewish education, and after his father – a famous teacher and writer as well – died, Shabazi moved to the large and beautiful city of Taiz. Situated in the Yemeni Highlands, Taiz had a

An aerial view of Shabazi Street and the Neve Tzedek neighborhood shot from the Shalom Tower, built in 1965. There's a stark contrast between that thirty-four-story building and the small, red-tiled roofs of the neighborhood's old homes.

Though originally a beautiful and prosperous neighborhood, Shabazi Street and the entire area experienced neglect and decay over time, as people moved to ever newer areas further north. All this changed with urban renewal efforts in the 1980s.

Shalom Shabazi (1619–ca. 1720)

A magnet for local and international visitors, these two-story colorful terracotta buildings are home to upscale eateries, galleries, jewelry and clothing boutiques, and of course bistros and cafés. More contemporary towers are seen as a backdrop to these small village-like streets.

This narrow cobblestoned street is the main artery of Neve Tzedek. Out of frame, but not out of mind, is the Suzanne Dellal Center for Dance and Theater, home of the internationally renowned Bat Sheva Dance Company.

Jewish presence dating back to 130 CE. At the foot of famous Mount Sabir, Shabazi built a synagogue and mikveh (ritual bath) to serve his followers.

From Taiz, Shabazi joined most of Yemen's Jews in their long trek and exile to Mawza. It is claimed that 20 percent of the community died during this era before being invited back to Yemen proper to continue to fulfill their designated role as cleaners of public sewers and latrines. They were also, rabbi and simple worker alike, responsible for cleaning animal feces and carcasses from marketplaces.

In addition to poetry, Shabazi also wrote a religious commentary in Hebrew, Aramaic, and Judeo-Arabic. Among his famous works, *Pleasant Days* is an interpretation of the Pentateuch. He wrote books on Kabbalah and astrology, and when word reached Yemen about Shabtai Zvi in 1666, he, like many troubled Jews, placed his hope in this so-called messianic figure and wrote about him. Shabazi also wrote about the return to the Jewish homeland. Though Shabazi's grave in Taiz is important to Jews and Muslims alike, the Israel government is trying to bring the great poet's remains to Israel, to fulfill his vision of return. His work is already here. The poems "If the Doors Are Locked" and "As'alk" are hit songs sung by numerous Israeli-Yemenite singers.

Shabazi Street is in the heart of the Neve Tzedek neighborhood. It is a narrow, winding street filled with cafés, elegant restaurants, galleries, and fashion and craft shops. Since being rédiscovered by artists in the 1980s, many of the small, late nineteenth-century buildings have been restored. When the Suzanne Dellal Center for Dance and Theater opened on Shabazi Street, the visibility of the village-like street skyrocketed.

CHAIM VITAL STREET

HIS WAS A LIFE LIVED among legends. One of the most famous Kabbalists of his day, Chaim Vital had the privilege of becoming the closest student to Rabbi Isaac Luria, "the Ari" (a Hebrew acronym for "the holy Rabbi Isaac"), soon after the master Kabbalist's arrival in Safed in 1570. For two years, until Luria's death, Vital remained by his teacher's side, learning the secrets and mysteries of the universe. Fortunately for posterity and the spiritual traditions of the Jewish world, Vital had the foresight to write down these extraordinary teachings.

Chaim Vital was born in the Galilee town of Safed in 1542. His father, Joseph, was a pious and learned man, a tefillin maker originally from Calabria, Italy. Even before he met the Ari, Chaim Vital was blessed with the company of exceptional teachers and Talmudic scholars, including Moshe Alsheikh, Joseph Caro, Shlomo Alkabetz, and Moshe Cordovero. Alongside his Jewish education, Vital studied alchemy, inspired by a dream he had in which he understood he was destined to become a learner and teacher of mysticism.

From writing down his teacher's words, Vital continued to write his own Kabbalistic commentaries. He began his first, *Seven Heavens*, after he moved to Damascus to become the religious leader for a community of Sicilian Jews. In this book, he wrote about the mystical and physical properties of the seven (known) planets and their seven corresponding metals.

An aerial view of the Florentine neighborhood from the 1940s when Sephardic immigrants from Europe filled the apartment blocks. The white plaster buildings were on par with those in neighborhoods south and north. In the 1940s, this area was the center of the paramilitary resistance group the Irgun Tzva'i Leumi, headed by Avraham Stern ("Yair"), who was caught and killed by the British Criminal Investigation Department.

Young men play soccer on the street in 1970. For many years, this working-class neighborhood was home to mostly Greek, Bulgarian, and North African Jews. When many began to move to more gentrified areas in the city, this neighborhood went into decline. Today, the Florentin neighborhood is one of the city's most desirable areas.

the Baal Shem Tov, and until today it is actively studied by students of Kabbalah.

Vital also wrote other important books about the universe and the human part in the cosmic drama. Among them are *The Treasure of Life*, *The Book of Reincarnation*, *The Book of Visions*, and *The Gates of Holiness*. He believed that learning Kabbalah was a gateway to messianic times.

In the middle of bohemian Florentin, Chaim Vital Street has the measure of two blocks and is as lively as the night is long. Famous for its side-by-side pubs and restaurants, it offers your fill of German beer, Mexican margaritas, and home-grown Mediterranean recipes. Complementing the appetite is the open-air gallery on the buildings' walls, featuring some of Tel Aviv's edgiest graffiti and street art.

A city-sponsored beautification project: garbage made useful. An old dumpster was creatively transformed into a garden of colorful flowers and plants on one side. On the other, benches are available for people walking along this heavily trafficked street.

But Vital is most famous for his eight-volume *Shemonah She'arim* (*Eight Gates*). Later published as *The Tree of Life*, this book is considered the most essential and approachable text on Lurianic Kabbalism. It discusses the divine order, the existence of matter, the perception of reality, and the mystically revealed/deduced structure of the universe. Believed by many to be the most important book of Jewish mysticism after the *Zohar*, it is often seen as an invaluable commentary on the *Zohar* itself. The opening lines indicate that only the most profound truths will be explored between its covers: "You know, before the beginning of the Creation, there was only the highest and fullest light. The description of the creation process starts precisely from that point." *The Tree of Life* inspired the eighteenth-century founder of Hasidism,

A neighborhood resident with her baby in a stroller and her dog on a leash walks in front of a wall of street art. This mural brings together images and messages about passion, love, and spirituality.

YAFO

IN THIS OLDEST AND MOST southern part of the city, there is a stimulating blend of cultures, religions, and eras. Not only does Yafo appear in both the Jewish and Christian Bibles, it is mentioned in the Egyptian Amarna tablets, which feature correspondence between the Egyptian government and its administrators in Canaan dating back to 1440 BCE. There was always plenty of action in the port city of Yafo; archeological digs have revealed how it was conquered, destroyed, and rebuilt many times over its long history. Yafo's oldest archeological evidence dates back to 7500 BCE.

In 1950, Yafo officially became a part of the Tel Aviv municipality. Since then, there has been a concerted effort to explore, excavate, and restore its many historic and religious sites. Yafo is home to a diverse set of churches, mosques, and synagogues, reflecting its heterogeneous population of Arabs and Jews of many ethnic backgrounds.

Ancient Yafo Port has also been transformed into a place of entertainment, while it remains a working fishing port. At dawn the boats go out, and by noon the fishermen return with the catch of the day, destined for the city's restaurants. On any given day, and especially on any given evening, the electric pulse of the crowd is all over the small streets and courtyards of the Old City, the square around the Ottoman Clock Tower (completed in 1903), the magnetic Flea Market selling bric-a-brac by day and alive with restaurants and bars by night, and the Noga District with the Gesher Theater as its center. Bustling galleries, shops, pubs, and cafés teem with people seeking enrichment and fun.

Yafo's northern entrance is known as Clock Tower Square for the Ottoman-era Clock Tower that acts as a beacon for this ancient part of the city. The restored marble pillars and arches on the left are what remain of the façade of the Saraya Building, once a Turkish governor's house. Opposite it, a Turkish jail, then an Israeli police station, has exotically morphed into an elegant boutique hotel.

RICHARD BEER-HOFMANN STREET

LIKE MANY CENTRAL EUROPEAN WRITERS of his generation, the Austrian Richard Beer-Hofmann wrote on the subjects of loneliness, the need for love and connection, and the anxiety of wondering if there was an ultimate meaning to life. Though he was an unaffiliated Jew who for decades downplayed this part of his identity, nevertheless among his best-known works were plays – *Jacob's Dream* (1918) and *Young David* (1933) – that used biblical themes not only to address these existential concerns, but to celebrate the Jews' ongoing connection to the ethical foundations of the Torah.

Born in Vienna to an assimilated Jewish family, Beer-Hofmann moved to Brno, the Czech Republic, with his aunt and uncle, who adopted him after the death of his mother. In 1880, he returned to Vienna, finished his schooling at the Akademisches Gymnasium, and went on to study law. Receiving his degree in 1890, he was set to join his father's law firm, but the art world of Vienna, specifically the writers and passion of the Young Vienna literary circle, grabbed his attention instead. Theodor Herzl, also a member of this group, tried but failed to interest Beer-Hofmann in Zionism. Herzl rebuked Beer-Hofmann and claimed he was ashamed of being a Jew. Beer-Hofmann responded by asking Herzl for the names of his children. "Pauline, Hans, and Trude, as you well know," was the response. "Mine are Miriam, Naema, and Gabriel, and my wife Paula has also taken on the biblical name Ruth," Beer-Hofmann said. Herzl conceded that his fellow writer was indeed a proud Jew.

Soon after Beer-Hofmann began writing plays, poetry, novellas, and criticism, he became one of the most respected writers of turn-of-the-century Viennese Modernism. His *Lullaby for Miriam*, written for his infant daughter in 1897, launched him into the spotlight of German letters. Using the well-known rhyme and rhythm of lullabies, Beer-Hofmann wrote about birth, loneliness, loss, and the ultimate

The Immanuel Church, designed by Paul Ferdinand Groth, was built in 1904. It served the German Evangelical community, including the Templars. The church was closed by British authorities in 1940, when many Germans were arrested as enemy nationals.

The German Colony in Yafo was made up of German Templars who came to the Holy Land to help usher in the Second Coming of Jesus. Founded in 1869, this settlement was their second in the country.

Richard Beer-Hofmann (1866–1945)

Old and new buildings and parks pepper the Noga District. This apartment building, while not new, has been renovated, and floors have been added to it. The renovation retains lovely period details: wooden shutters over long, thin windows and decorative balcony railings.

Colony – founded in the nineteenth century by Christian believers from Maine – Beer-Hofmann Street has numerous building styles on it, from America's New England wooden houses to stone-clad Ottoman. Rising proudly at number 15, the Neo-Gothic Lutheran Immanuel Church dates from 1904. It possesses the largest church organ in the country.

challenge – that of death. The tension between the childish form and grown-up content was original and thought-provoking.

Though in 1905, Beer-Hofmann received the prestigious German prize the Volks-Schillerpreis, in 1933, his work was banned in Nazi Germany. As years passed, Beer-Hofmann became more identified with his Judaism, and in 1936 he visited Palestine. In 1939, when the dangers could no longer be ignored, Beer-Hofmann fled Vienna for the United States. Tragically, his wife died en route. In 1945, Beer-Hofmann became a U.S. citizen and received the Distinguished Achievements Award from the National Institute of the American Academy of Arts and Letters. Later that year, he died in New York City.

Beer-Hofmann Street is part of the Noga District behind the Gesher Theater, whose network of small streets is filled with shops and homes of artists and designers. Originally part of the Yafo American

The old house on the left is in dire need of restoration. Who knows if it will survive the city's demand for multistory housing. A large park at the end of the street provides a welcome green relief to area residents.

YEHUDA MERAGUSA STREET

YAFO'S FIRST RABBI, YEHUDA HALEVI MERAGUSA, was a very early Zionist who moved to Ottoman Palestine in 1801. He believed in the Jewish people's return to their ancient homeland, as he believed in coexistence with the other people living in the land and that Jews had to be economically self-sufficient to thrive in their old-new homeland.

Born Raphael Yehuda Ben Menachem Halevi in Sarajevo, he had a traditional Jewish education in the Croatian city of Ragusa. He moved in 1801 to Jerusalem, where he studied Torah for another eighteen years before assuming his lifelong vocation as a rabbi. He moved to Yafo, set

down roots, and in 1840 was appointed rabbi by the Sephardic rabbis in Jerusalem. This was no small matter, for it reflected the resurgence in the city of the Jewish community, which had been pretty much decimated by the bubonic plague decades earlier.

Meragusa (a nickname given to him by the Bohemian-Austrian writer Ludwig August Frankl when they met in 1855 – it means "from Ragusa"), believed that Jews had to return to the land, not only as devotees but as farmers. Meragusa bought land and planted orange groves, like his Arab neighbors. He also encouraged his growing congregation to learn other

This beautiful panorama of Yafo, taken in the 1940s, shows the Clock Ttower and behind it, the Ottoman-era Saraya (municipality building). On Meragusa Street (out of the frame to the right) stands the Yafo Cemetery, consecrated in 1839 and active until 1920. Yehuda Meragusa, who died in 1879, was buried here.

Yehuda Meragusa (1783–1879)

This corner establishment offers residents and visitors some of the best gelato and ice cream east of Italy. Israelis consume enormous quantities of ice cream, in creative flavors that reflect the rich, diverse, and fine local culinary culture.

Right next to the Flea Market, one of many food establishments to stop in for an espresso, a coffee and pastry, or a full two-to-three-course meal that culls its farm-to-sea-to-table ingredients from the local produce market and fishermen.

skills that would promote independence, such as smithing and carpentry. Despite rabbinical resistance, Meragusa persisted and was able to convince Moses Montefiore of the soundness of this enterprise. Montefiore was convinced and in 1855 bought a citrus grove from Meragusa, though the rabbi continued to cultivate and manage it.

Fluent in Hebrew, Arabic, Ladino, Serbian, French, and Turkish, Meragusa was respected by all the residents of Yafo, regardless of ethnic or religious background. Known for his wisdom and graciousness, he was honored by many. In 1863, Meragusa established the Yafo City Committee, and together, Sephardim and Ashkenazim actively recruited funds to open the local branch of the Alliance Israélite Universelle. Here, boys received a solid basic education in academic and farming skills. In later years, at age ninety, he traveled to Egypt to solicit funds for a yeshiva in Yafo.

Just as Meragusa campaigned hard to bring schools to his community, so too did he recognize that a living community also needed a place to bury their dead. "Death is a part of life," Meragusa explained before founding the cemetery that enabled Jews to avoid having to travel to Jerusalem for funerals. This small cemetery, home to about eight hundred graves and in which he is buried, on the corner of Meragusa Street and Yehuda HaYamit Street, held its last burial in 1986.

In the heart of the Old City of Yafo, Yehuda Meragusa Street touches the lively, colorful, and very popular Flea Market. Filled with second-hand shops selling anything and everything, in recent years the street along with the area has gone through a serious facelift: apartment buildings, hotels, and many restaurants, cafés, and pubs turn the street into a magnet for fun and frolic come dusk.

DAVID RAZIEL STREET

AT A YOUNG AGE, DAVID RAZIEL heard the calling to fight and lead. Though his life was tragically short, he left a strong imprint on the armed struggle for Jewish sovereignty. A founder and eventual commander in chief of the Irgun Tzva'i Leumi, Raziel devoted himself entirely to the destiny of the Jewish people. Honored as a modern Jewish warrior, Raziel lived and died by the sword.

Born David Rozenson in 1910 in Russia, Raziel moved to Ottoman Palestine with his family when he was three years old. He had a secular upbringing and studied philosophy and mathematics at the Hebrew University in Jerusalem. There he met fellow student Abraham Stern, who introduced him to Jewish practices and the religious Zionist philosophy of Palestine's Ashkenazi chief rabbi, Abraham Isaac Kook. In

1929, when Arab riots broke out in the country, he decided to leave his university studies to fight with the Haganah, a Jewish paramilitary organization. Two years later, when the more right-wing Irgun paramilitary organization was established, Raziel joined. He quickly showed military acumen and leadership skills. Within a few years, he was the commander of the Jerusalem District, and a year after that, commander in chief of the entire Irgun.

Raziel thought that the struggle with the country's Arabs was the more serious conflict that Jews in Palestine faced. His friend Stern felt otherwise, seeing the British as the obstacle to Jewish sovereignty. When World War II began, Raziel decided that Jews had to align themselves with the British in the fight against the Nazis. Over the years, he and

Saraya House and Howard Hotel are on the right in this late 1920s photograph by Frank Scholten. A small portion of stone carving remains from the hotel, including the inscription "Peace unto Israel." The House of Sursuk, at far left, still stands today.

A caravan of camels carries merchandise through Bustrus Street to or from Yafo Port. Dizengoff's first offices (for his import-export business), the Anglo-Palestine Bank, and the offices of Eretz Israel (a branch of the World Zionist Organization in Palestine) all lined this very busy thoroughfare.

David Raziel (1910–1941)

Stern moved farther away from each other's ideological positions, and a complete rift occurred in 1940. Stern left the Irgun and established the even more right-wing Freedom Fighters for Israel, aka Lehi.

As part of his commitment to work with the British Army, in 1941 Raziel traveled to Iraq with three other Irgun members to fight government forces aligned with the Axis powers. When a German plane bombed them, Raziel was killed. It took Raziel's widow, Shoshana, many years before she could bring his body to rest in Israel. But her persistence paid off, and in 1955, Raziel's remains were moved from Iraq to Cyprus, and from there to Jerusalem's military cemetery on Mount Herzl in 1961. Raziel was posthumously promoted to the rank of general.

David Raziel Street begins as the extension of Eilat Street (the border of Tel Aviv and Yafo) and ends at Clock Square at the northern entrance to Yafo. The Clock Tower is one of the defining elements of the Yafo skyline. Governor's House at number 21, built in 1880, was one of the first buildings built outside Yafo proper. Along the street and square, one finds buildings from the Ottoman and British periods with arches, narrow balconies, delicate ironwork, and other decorative elements. In spots, new construction has replaced the old, and once-vacant lots are filled with modern residences.

East meets West in this apartment building. Brown brick façade, decorative stone arches, floor-to-ceiling European windows, transoms, wooden shutters, and small Juliet balconies. This building reflects its many years and many owners, each with a unique aesthetic.

One of the most famous landmarks in the city. The brainchild of Jewish clockmaker Schoenberg, the Clock Tower was completed in 1903. Celebrating the twenty-five-year reign of Ottoman Sultan Abdul Hamid II, Yafo's Arabs and Jewish residents paid for it.

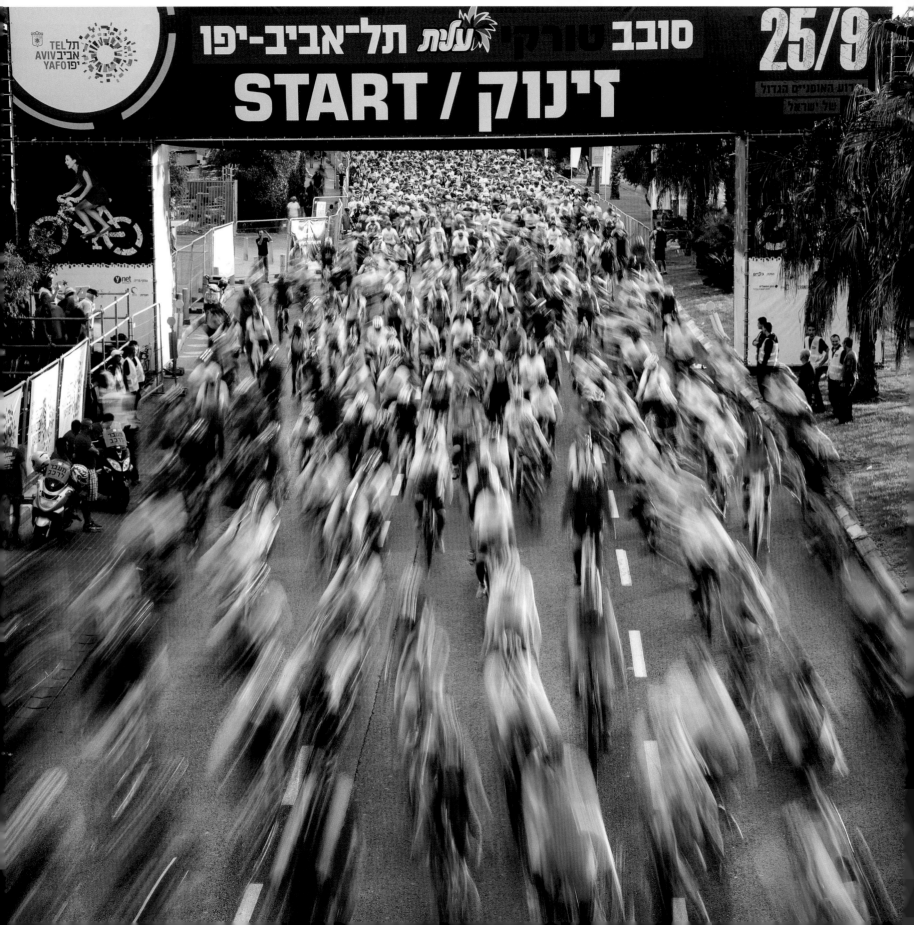

RAMAT AVIV AND NORTHERN ENVIRONS

THE RESIDENTIAL NEIGHBORHOODS NORTH OF the Yarkon River are filled with attractive contemporary high-rise buildings, gardens, wide streets, and as its residents like to boast, plenty of parking! Ramat Aviv was the first among the neighborhoods to be developed in the 1950s, and though it represents progress and modernity, archeological building remains dating back eight thousand years have been discovered here, including a Bronze Age burial cave, showing that this was not the first time people crossed the river for quality living.

Ramat Aviv's anchor projects were the Land of Israel Museum, followed by the world-recognized Tel Aviv University campus with its diverse student body. Over the years, other important cultural institutions moved into the neighborhood, namely the Museum of the Jewish People at Beit Hatfutsot, the Palmach Museum, and most recently the Yitzhak Rabin Center. But Ramat Aviv is not all work and no play. Not to be outdone by malls south of the Yarkon River, the Ramat Aviv Mall opened in 1997 and established its reputation for elegance and high-end shopping. To date, it remains the most expensive mall in the country.

To the east, Ramat Hachayal was established in 1949 for demobilized soldiers and was expanded in 1954 for Jews fleeing Shanghai, China. Commercial areas have sprouted from its predominantly residential streets, and the neighborhood is proudly shared with numerous high-tech companies, media companies, and Assuta Medical Center, the largest private hospital in the country. The new buildings of Ramat Aviv never seem to stop sprouting up.

Tel Aviv's annual Cycling Marathon, with different riding routes according to age and ability. Israelis come from all over the country to ride and to cheer. All routes take participants through many of the top spots of the city.

ALBERT EINSTEIN STREET

Imagination is more important than knowledge. Knowledge is limited. Imagination encircles the world. A.E.

THIS IS BUT ONE OF many celebrated quotes that Albert Einstein shared with the world. Most famous for reshaping concepts of how the universe works through his theories of relativity, Einstein was a man of many talents and interests, among them music, socialism, and Zionism. His intellectual capabilities were so tremendous that the name Einstein has become a code word for genius. His equation $E=MC^2$ changed the way scientists understood reality.

Born in Germany to a secular family, at age six Einstein attended a Catholic elementary school and began his lifelong love affair with music. He was an average pupil, not showing any of the potentials that would burst into the world as a young man. He dropped out of high school and eventually received a teaching degree from a technical school. When he could not find a teaching position, he left Germany for Zurich and studied at the Swiss Federal Polytechnic. Eventually, he moved to Bern to work in a patent office. During the seven years in that office, Einstein developed his Special Theory of Relativity and published four papers that made him famous. For them, he was awarded a PhD by the University of Zurich in 1905.

Eventually, Einstein returned to live in Germany and joined the Berlin Academy of Sciences. In 1921 he received a Nobel Prize in Physics for, as the committee wrote, "his services to theoretical physics, and especially for his discovery of the law of the photoelectric effect." In 1933 Einstein was in the United States when Hitler rose to power. When he decided to remain, the Institute for Advanced Study at Princeton University offered him a permanent appointment. Einstein lived and worked there for the rest of his life. Overall, he published nearly five hundred scientific and non-scientific papers and commented on many aspects of life, far beyond those of his scientific expertise.

Einstein became an American citizen in 1940 and supported the push to research nuclear fission and build an atom bomb. Eventually, though, he came out publicly against the use of such weapons, though they were built with the help of his theories. Einstein was a Zionist who supported the creation of the State of Israel and its institutions. He was instrumental in establishing the Hebrew University in Jerusalem and sat on its first board of governors. In 1952, he was asked to become president of the State of Israel but declined.

Throughout his life, Einstein played the violin and listened to music. He said it was the source of his greatest joy, and from it, he learned that when it comes to mastering a subject or skill, "love is a better teacher than a sense of duty." A socialist and an internationalist, Einstein was suspicious of nation-states' abuse of power. He died in Princeton, New Jersey, in 1955.

Utilitarian design, large balconies, and pilotis (piers), some of the elements of Bauhaus design, are incorporated here in these apartment blocks along the new, wide street. Fields spread out behind and beyond this cluster of buildings.

Albert Einstein (1879–1955)

Albert Einstein Street, in the Ramat Aviv neighborhood, is a wide boulevard that begins at the sea and ends at Tel Aviv University's campus. It is lined with residential buildings, student dorms, and the fashionable Ramat Aviv Mall.

Mural of the man Chaim Weizmann called "the greatest Jew alive." Though he was outspoken politically, Einstein declined Weizmann's offer to become the State of Israel's second president. Einstein claimed he was too old (seventy-three), too inexperienced, and lacked people skills.

This busy boulevard runs perpendicular to the beach, bringing sea air into the streets. Up ahead is the Tel Aviv University campus. To the right, out of frame, but not out of reach, is the fashionable Ramat Aviv Mall.

This large metal sculpture outside the Sea Gate entrance of the mall represents motion. A tall, long metal cylinder loops around and ends with an airplane tail inside a metal spiral and behind an old locomotive façade and chimney.

LEVI ESHKOL BOULEVARD

LEVI ESHKOL WORE MANY HATS. He was a farmer, a soldier, an economist, and a politician. The third prime minister of Israel (fourth if one counts Ben-Gurion's non-consecutive terms separately), Eshkol left a lasting and robust mark on Israel's destiny. He was instrumental in raising desperately needed funds to support the country's developing infrastructure and its absorption of hundreds of thousands of immigrants. A decade later, in the 1960s, he also established a close and strategic relationship with the United States.

Born Levi Shkolnik in the Ukraine in 1895, Eshkol received a traditional Jewish education, which included a move to Vilnius, Lithuania, for yeshiva studies. While there, at age sixteen, he also joined the Youth of Zion youth group, which marked the beginning of his political consciousness and activism. Three years later, at nineteen, he moved to Ottoman Palestine and worked in farming and became a member of the Judea Worker's Union. He volunteered with the British Army's Jewish Legion during World War I and in 1920 became a founding member of Kibbutz Degania Bet near the Sea of Galilee.

When the resistance to British rule became more focused, Eshkol joined the Haganah paramilitary organization. He became a commander not long after and was tasked with raising funds for weapons. It wasn't such a stretch then from these years of experience to his appointment as director-general of the Ministry of Defense in 1950. When Eshkol was elected a Knesset member in 1951, he was made finance minister, a position he held for twelve years. When Ben-Gurion resigned as prime minister in 1963, Eshkol, as per Ben-Gurion's request, was elected Mapai Party chairman and became prime minister.

In 1964, after a decade of planning and construction, the National Water Carrier system in Israel opened under Eshkol's watch. Unfortunately, the economic growth that enabled this soon collapsed, and Eshkol's economic policies did little at the time to help increasing

Workers building the runway of the Dov Hoz Airport (also called Sde Dov Airport, officially closed in 2019) near Eshkol Street in 1938. The airport also served as an air force base. The air base served mostly domestic flights as well as Cyprus.

Children play in a large pile of sand belonging to the building sites seen behind them. Sand and lye make the plaster that clads the buildings. Sand and cement make concrete. Sand, plentiful throughout Israel, particularly in Tel Aviv, is an essential construction material in the country.

Levi Eshkol (1895–1969)

unemployment and inflation. Years later, they helped the country recover and stabilize financially. But Eshkol's great achievement in the field of foreign relations did not suffer extreme ups and downs. West Germany, the Soviet Union, and the United States were three of the enormously influential countries with whom Eshkol worked to establish diplomatic and working ties. President Lyndon Johnson's special relationship with Eshkol was fateful; if not for American military support during the Six-Day War in 1967, Israel might not have been able to win. A year and a half later, in 1969, Eshkol suffered a fatal heart attack. He was the first prime minister to die in office and was given a statesman's funeral on Mount Herzl in Jerusalem.

Levi Eshkol Boulevard runs parallel to the sea in Ramat Aviv from Rokach Boulevard all the way north to Propes Street. It is an important parallel north-south route to Namir Road (Highway 2) within sight of the sea. Filled with new multistoried residential buildings, the multilane boulevard's middle island boasts tall palm trees and grass.

The westernmost boulevard in northern Tel Aviv celebrates Independence Day with flags unfurled. Today, it is home to thousands and an important option to the highway and other north-south roads when the going gets rough during rush hour.

ABBA KOVNER STREET

Let us not go like lambs to the slaughter. True, we are weak and without defense, but the only answer to the enemy is resistance. Brothers! Better fall as free fighters than live at our murderers' mercy! A.K.

THIS FAMOUS QUOTE BY ABBA KOVNER captures the spirit of Jewish resistance during World War II, while the image of sheep to slaughter has endured as a symbol of a people so beaten down they were unable to imagine – let alone carry out – fighting against their annihilation. Kovner didn't buy into that image. From the Vilna Ghetto to a partisan fighting unit in the Lithuanian forests, from the Haganah to the Israel Defense Forces, Kovner lived his philosophy. When he did lay down his arms, he took up the pen and continued to embody modern Jewish heroism through potent and major poems about his people's suffering, destiny, and empowerment.

Born in the Black Sea city of Sevastopol, Russia, in 1918, Kovner grew up in Vilnius and was educated both in Jewish texts and in the arts. Though related to the famous nineteenth-century Rabbi Elijah of Vilna, aka the Vilna Gaon (genius), as a teenager, Kovner joined the Young Guard, a socialist, secular Zionist movement. There he first learned that Jews could take their destinies into their own hands.

In 1941, when Germany invaded Vilnius and the Jews were moved into the ghetto, Kovner helped organize resistance, first inside the ghetto and then from outside, following his escape to the woods. He was part of the core that formed the United Partisan Organization targeting German soldiers and local forces. Taking significant risks, Kovner would slip in and out of the ghetto to organize fighting cells there. In 1944, when Vilnius was liberated by the Russian army, Kovner founded the Escape Movement to enable Jews to leave eastern Europe. And when World War II ended, he moved to Palestine and joined the Haganah. From there it was a natural transition to the Israeli army, where he became a captain in the Givati Brigade.

In 1946, Kovner became a member of Kibbutz Ein HaHoresh and began to write. His first book of poetry, *Until There Is No Light*, was published in 1947 and recounts the partisan battles. Two books of prose and numerous poetry volumes were published after that, mostly about the Jewish fight in Europe and Israel. In 1961, Kovner testified at the Adolf Eichmann trial in Tel Aviv and recognized the importance of this public naming of Jewish suffering. It was "like a dam that has been burst," he wrote, "the sealed hearts of many [...] Holocaust survivors [have] been opened, and there is no home where someone did not speak out his most hidden memories." In 1970, Kovner received the Israel Prize for Literature. He also helped found the Museum of the Jewish People

Abba Kovner, a witness for the prosecution, during his testimony at the trial of Nazi war criminal Adolf Eichmann, held at Beit Ha'Am in Jerusalem, 1961.

Abba Kovner (1918–1987)

and designed the permanent exhibition's thematic layout. Kovner died at his kibbutz in 1987.

Abba Kovner Street in the North Star area of Ramat Aviv is lovely and residential, filled with tall modern apartments and beautifully manicured gardens and traffic islands.

The streets and residents in the northern edge of the Kochav HaTzafon (North Star) neighborhood are getting ready for Independence Day. Strung along lampposts and from the roofs of the tall buildings, Israeli flags wave joyfully in the breeze.

A Silk Floss Tree holds court in a traffic circle. Known by the botanical name Chorisa speciosa, this beauty hails from Paraguay and northern Argentina. Covered top to bottom in thorns, it is animal resistant and gets by on little water.

At a Hotel

Mother and Father begin to die within me.
Thirty years after their stormy death
they steal away quietly from my rooms
and my hours of grace.

I know for sure the voices have ceased
and things are free. And bearing no grudge,
they will no longer visit my home. After all
a living man needs to stand here alone.
Somewhere.

Father wakes up now, shuffles in his sandals
and as usual pretends he doesn't see
how mother wipes her tears
as she knits a warm sweater
for her son on his way, at the way station.

Translated by Karen Alkalay-Gut

CHAIM LEVANON STREET

THE SIXTH MAYOR OF TEL AVIV, Chaim Levanon devoted many years to developing the cultural and social life of his beloved city. His crowning achievement was the consolidation of Tel Aviv University, planning its location on a new pastoral campus in the city's northern neighborhood of Ramat Aviv.

Born Chaim Yosef Levinstein in Poland, Levanon had a traditional Jewish education but also a secular one. At Cracow's Jagiellonian University, he studied engineering and agriculture before moving to British Mandate Palestine at twenty-eight. His commitment to education started as a teacher at the Ahad Ha'am Gymnasium in Petah Tikva, and political activism led to the founding of the General Zionist movement, whose moderate right-leaning ideology emphasized individual aspirations and private enterprise. Eventually, Levanon became secretary-general of the movement's labor union, a good training ground

The opening of Haaretz Museum in 1956. Today, known as MUSA (Museum of Eretz Israel), this is a sprawling museum, focusing on Israeli culture, archaeology, ethnography, and Israeli arts and crafts.

Bird's-eye view of the Ramat Aviv neighborhood showing Chaim Levanon Street (originally known as University Street) at the bottom, 1964.

for the more rigorous leadership he would need to run the growing metropolis of Tel Aviv from 1953 to 1959.

Levanon was first a member of the Tel Aviv City Council. Then as deputy mayor of Tel Aviv under Israel Rokach, he learned more about the day-to-day running of the city. Finally, when Rokach became minister of the interior in the national government, the city council appointed Levanon as acting mayor. Two years later, in 1955, he won the position in municipal elections, a post he then held until 1959. As mayor, Levanon changed the face of Tel Aviv. He helped pave the way for the construction of the Mann Auditorium and the Helena Rubinstein Pavilion of the Tel Aviv Museum of Art. Attentive to neighborhood needs, he had playgrounds and schools built and had the city take responsibility for children's summer camps. But his outstanding achievement was the integration of the various faculties of Tel Aviv University into one home, on one campus. Levanon oversaw the laying of the cornerstone

for the School of Law and Economics in 1955, the first university building on the Ramat Aviv campus.

In 1973, Levanon was honored with the key to the city, and upon his death in 1986, he was equally honored with a burial in Trumpeldor Cemetery, a Who's Who of prominent figures in Tel Aviv's and Israel's history.

Chaim Levanon Street in Ramat Aviv, aptly enough, sparkles with cultural institutions. It begins on Namir Road and ends on Keren Kayemet Boulevard, curving past the Eretz Israel Museum, the Palmach Museum, Reidman College, the Rabin Center, and the large beautiful campus of Tel Aviv University that Levanon helped shepherd into the world.

Planetarium located among the twenty acres of the multidisciplinary Eretz Israel (Land of Israel) Museum. The renovated, state-of-the-art planetarium has a revolving stage to better see a simulation of the stars and galaxies of our night sky, among other alluring attractions.

Tel Aviv University has most of its main entrances off this artery. Since its founding in 1956, students from the area and from all over the country come to study here, making it the largest university in the country.

ISRAEL ROKACH BOULEVARD

FOR SEVENTEEN YEARS, ISRAEL ROKACH was the second mayor of Tel Aviv. He so loved the city that he named his youngest daughter Iri (my city). From 1936 to 1953, under Rokach's guiding hand, the city of Tel Aviv became the largest Jewish city in the country, tripling in population, and a model for self-governance, cultural development, and immigrant absorption. In 1950, when Yafo became part of Tel Aviv, Rokach coined its new name: Tel Aviv-Yafo.

Born in the neighborhood of Neve Tzedek in 1886, Israel Rokach had a traditional Jewish education before attending Yafo's Alliance High School. His father, a journalist, was among the founders of Neve Tzedek, and his grandfather was instrumental in establishing the country's Hebrew printing industry. No wonder Rokach's connection to the land and to Hebrew culture and language was so great. He studied electrical engineering in Switzerland so that he would be able to help build electric plants to advance Israel's technological and economic future.

But history and politics interfered. When Rokach returned to what was now British Mandate Palestine, instead of electric plants, he opened an electrical supply store in Yafo and became involved in local politics. First, he was a city council member in Yafo, then a council member in Tel Aviv. In 1929, Rokach became deputy mayor of Tel Aviv and worked very closely with Mayor Meir Dizengoff. When Dizengoff died in office seven years later, Rokach was appointed mayor, a choice favored by the British, who made sure Rokach remained in that role when elections were held later that year. But ironies abound. Rokach was not a yes-man, and he resisted British policies when it came to Jewish immigration and defense. He was among a group of political leaders imprisoned by the British in 1947 for helping the Jewish paramilitary undergrounds. Yet years later, the British awarded him the title of Officer of the Order of the British Empire for all the work he did for the city of Tel Aviv.

Mayor Dizengoff with his deputy mayor, Israel Rokach. In 1936, when Dizengoff died, Rokach succeeded him as mayor, a post he held until 1953.

Tel Aviv's only drive-in theater opened in 1973, and its first screening was Walt Disney's Jungle Book. *Abandoned for years, it was revived in 2020 during the COVID-19 pandemic.*

Israel Rokach (1886–1959)

During his many years in office, much of the infrastructure of the growing city was laid down, including immigrant housing, constructing the urban grid and parks designed by Sir Patrick Geddes in the 1920s, and building bomb shelters and a public announcement system. Rokach was a member of Knesset from 1948 until his death. When he was appointed minister of the interior in 1953, however, he had to leave the office of mayor. Rokach died in 1959 and like many important national luminaries was buried in the city's landmark Trumpeldor Cemetery.

Rokach Boulevard starts near the western bend of the Yarkon River and runs parallel to it for many kilometers until it curves north and ends straddling Ganei Yehoshua Yarkon Park on one side and the Tel Aviv Exhibition Grounds on the other. Where Rokach Boulevard hugs the Yarkon Park, it offers a vista of green lawns, trees, bodies of water, and playgrounds for all ages. Of particular note is the Daniel Rowing Center at number 2 with its distinct nautical building design.

Ganei Hataaruchah Merkaz Hayeridim (The Fair Gardens Convention Center) is one of the country's major venues for conferences and business and art fairs. Opened in a different location in 1932, it was renamed in 2018 and is known as Expo Tel Aviv.

Right: Busking for a shekel. This pair of street jugglers-acrobats-clowns show off their considerable skills for drivers waiting at a red light. They need to get through their act and go car to car for donations before the light turns green.

SHAI AGNON STREET

SHMUEL YOSEF AGNON IS ONE of modern Hebrew's most important writers. His language, choice of subject, and breadth of knowledge in Judaic and European cultures earned him a Nobel Prize for Literature in 1966 – the only Hebrew writer to be so honored. Agnon's work is steeped in tradition, yet reaches toward the future with modern ironies and twists that reflect the alienation of the twentieth-century individual.

Born Shmuel Yosef Halevi Czaczkes in 1888, in today's Ukraine, Agnon was homeschooled in religious texts, works of the Jewish Enlightenment, and in German, which in later years opened to him modern European literature and thought. Beginning his writing career at the tender age of eight, at fifteen he published his first Yiddish-language poem about the legendary medieval mystic Joseph della Reina.

What interested Agnon as a religious writer was how a traditional identity and lifestyle intersected with the pressures and realities of secular society, both in Europe and in Ottoman Palestine, to where he moved in 1908. The first story he published, "Chained Wives" ("Agunot" in Hebrew), became the inspiration for his pen name, Agnon. Just as a "chained wife" whose husband won't grant her a *get* (Jewish divorce) is caught between being married and yet not living as married, this name reflected Agnon's sense of being caught between worlds – Europe and Israel, religious and secular, dreams and realities. His first name also

In 1966, the Nobel Prize in Literature was shared by the fiction writer S.Y. Agnon and the poet Nellie Sachs. A candid moment is captured when Sachs adjusts Agnon's tie before they go on stage to receive this great honor.

underwent a change, though this was from the Hebrew reading public who contracted the S and Y of his first two names and called him Shai (meaning "gift" in Hebrew).

Agnon left Palestine and lived in Germany from 1913 to 1924. There he experienced two enormously important partnerships: he met and married his wife, Esther Marx, and he met the publisher Salman Schocken,

"There was an old woman in Jerusalem. An attractive old woman the likes of which you've never seen. She was holy and she was wise and she was modest and graceful. The light in her eyes was of kindness and mercy, and the wrinkles in her face, blessings and peace. Were it not impossible to compare women to angels, then I would compare her to an angel of God. And this, too, she had – a maiden's spryness. Were it not for garments of the elderly on her, no other trace of old age was about her."

Opening paragraph of the short story "Tehillah," in *Ad Henah*, by Shai Agnon, © Schocken, 1952, all rights reserved

Shai Agnon (1888–1970)

who became his publisher and literary patron. When Agnon returned to British Mandate Palestine, he settled in the Talpiot neighborhood of Jerusalem and continued to write. Overall, he would produce twenty-four books that were translated into over eighteen languages. His 1931 novel *The Bridal Canopy* was hailed as a masterpiece, only to be followed by the novella *A Simple Story* in 1935, and *Only Yesterday* in 1945, often called the Great Hebrew Novel. These books cemented his reputation not only as a stylist, but as a writer able to weave together a wide range of Jewish history, thought, and experience.

Twice Agnon received the Bialik Prize for Literature (in 1934 and 1950) and twice the Israel Prize for Literature (in 1954 and 1958). He was so respected that when he complained about traffic noise near his house, the Jerusalem municipality closed his street to cars with a sign at the entrance that read: "No entry to vehicles, writer at work." Agnon died in Jerusalem in 1970, and his home has become a museum honoring his life and work.

Shai Agnon Street is wide and long in the North Star section of the Ramat Aviv neighborhood. Tall modern apartment buildings line the street, and its traffic islands are grassy and dotted with lovely palm trees starting on Namir Road and on to Ibn Gabirol.

Wheels, wheels, wheels... Tel Avivians love their bicycles and their skooters, be they smartly electric or conventional using muscle and grit. Girlfriends ride side saddle. Dogs run alongside their people keeping up, keeping in shape.

Going west-east from the beach to busy Namir Road. This most northern thoroughfare before the Reading Power Station and now defunct Sde Dov Airport brings beauty to the eye with a median filled with colorful seasonal flowers and towering trees.

RAOUL WALLENBERG STREET

ISRAEL'S RIGHTEOUS AMONG THE NATIONS count Raoul Wallenberg as one of their own. Devoted to helping Hungarian Jews escape the vice grip of the Nazi occupation, Wallenberg eventually paid for his humanitarian rescues with his own life. To this day, his fate has never been clarified, with some believing he died in prison at the hands of the Russians, who suspected him of spying for the United States.

While the Soviet authorities were not entirely wrong, nor were they right. Wallenberg, who was born in Stockholm, Sweden, spent his college years at the University of Michigan studying architecture. After this junket, he moved to South Africa to work for a Swedish building firm and then moved to Palestine, where he was employed by a Dutch banking firm in Haifa. Upon his return to Sweden, Wallenberg went into business with Koloman Lauer, a Hungarian Jew, who needed a non-Jew free to travel throughout Nazi-occupied Europe selling his company's gourmet food products. All this international business experience prepared Wallenberg for the last and most courageous six-month chapter of his life: working in Budapest as Sweden's special envoy with the explicit goal of saving Hungarian Jewry.

The passports Wallenberg issued provided thousands of Jews with safe passage out of Hungary. Wallenberg also used the extra-territorial Swedish embassy as a refuge for Jews. The compelling question is what motivates a person to risk his life under such perilous circumstances. What is known is that during his months working in Haifa, he

Philip Jackson's bronze monument to Raoul Wallenberg stands outside the Western Marble Arch Synagogue and in close proximity to the Swedish embassy in London. His right hand clutches several Schutzpassen secreted away beneath his open coat. Wallenberg used these passes to save Hungarian Jews. The monument was unveiled in 1997 by Queen Elizabeth II.

On September 30, 1944, Raoul Wallenberg signed this work pass for Julie Heller, designating her a necessary functionary of the Swedish embassy and thereby saving her life. For six months, when Wallenberg was Sweden's special envoy to Hungary, he saved thousands of Jews by issuing them passports and embassy work passes and protecting them in buildings that he declared had extraterritorial diplomatic immunity.

Raoul Wallenberg (1912–1952?)

met Jews who had escaped Germany, whose stories had a profound effect on him. Some speculate that his grandmother's Jewish grandfather brought this suffering closer to home. But whatever the reason, in 1944 when asked to work for the US War Refugee Board in Hungary to help Jews escape, Wallenberg rose to the occasion. The Swedes gave him diplomatic status and the use of an embassy building, and he set to work rescuing Jews. But it was his association with the Americans that sealed his fate.

When the Red Army entered Budapest, Wallenberg was arrested as an American spy and disappeared into the Soviet penal system. Some speculate that he died in the notorious KGB Lubyanka Prison in Moscow in 1947. Some reports claim he was sighted alive after this, though still a prisoner. In any event, he was never seen or heard from again in the West. To acknowledge his humanitarian work, Wallenberg was made an honorary citizen of the United States in 1981, and in 2012 was posthumously awarded a Congressional Gold Medal. He has also been granted honorary citizenship in Canada, Hungary, Australia, and Israel.

Raoul Wallenberg Street is a main artery in Tel Aviv's northeastern neighborhood of Ramat Hachayal. Assuta Medical Center, one of the largest and most prestigious private hospitals in central Israel, is located on this new broad street, with commercial traffic and tree-lined blocks.

Teenagers practice twists and jumps in front of Ziviel House in Ramat Hachayal. Established in 1949 for demobilized soldiers and war widows, in recent decades this northeastern area of the city has become a hub for high tech, development, and media companies.

Planted around a tall office building, these young trees have had their trunks hauntingly painted white to protect them from cracking and splitting, which can lead to disease and insects. So while the white paint is practical, it's also beautiful.

CREDITS

Texts

p. 47 *bottom right:* Hannah Semer, *God Doesn't Live Here Anymore* [Hebrew] (Tel Aviv: Dvir, 1995). We wish to thank Professor Shlomith D. Zuta, daughter of Hannah Semer, for her kind permission to use these materials.

p. 52 *top:* Shaul Tchernichovsky, "I Believe," written in Odessa, 1892, translated from Hebrew by Vivian Eden, used with the permission of *Haaretz*

p. 119 *bottom right:* "At a Hotel" by Abba Kovner, translated by and used with the permission of Karen Alkalay-Gut, with kind permission from Michael Kovner

p. 124 *bottom:* S.Y. Agnon, opening paragraph of short story "Tehillah," originally published in Hebrew in *Ad Henah*, by Shai Agnon (Tel Aviv: Schocken, 1952), © Schocken, 1952, all rights reserved, translated by Miryam Sivan

Photos

All modern color photos are copyright © Ziv Koren, all rights reserved.

p. 2 *bottom right:* Arie Ilan Collection, Yad Ben-Zvi Photo Archives
bottom left: Detroit Publishing Co., catalogue J foreign section, Detroit, Mich.: Detroit Photographic Company, 1905, Library of Congress Prints and Photographs Division, Washington, DC

p. 3 *top:* Avraham Soskin, Soskin Collection, MUSA, Eretz Israel Museum, Tel Aviv

p. 4 *left:* Tel Aviv-Yafo Municipal Archives

pp. 4–5 *center:* Matson Photo Service, G. Eric and Edith Matson Photograph Collection, Library of Congress Prints and Photographs Division, Washington, DC, https://hdl.loc.gov/loc.pnp/res.258.mats

p. 5 *bottom right:* Matson Photo Service, G. Eric and Edith Matson Photograph Collection, Library of Congress Prints and Photographs Division, Washington, DC, https://hdl.loc.gov/loc.pnp/pp.print

p. 6 *bottom:* Willem van de Poll, National Archives of the Netherlands

p. 7 *top right:* Willem van de Poll, National Archives of the Netherlands

p. 10 *bottom right:* Zoltan Kluger, GPO National Photo Collection
bottom left: by kind permission of the Tel-Aviv Encyclopedia, www.tlv100.net

p. 11 *top right:* Zvi Oron, Central Zionist Archives

p. 12 *bottom left:* Itzhak Berez, courtesy of the Jabotinsky Institute in Israel

p. 13 *top right:* Yaacov Saar, GPO National Photo Collection, 1974

p. 14 *top right:* Rudi Weissenstein, The PhotoHouse Collection
bottom right: Zoltan Kluger, GPO National Photo Collection

p. 15 *top right:* Fritz Cohen, GPO National Photo Collection, 1968

p. 16 *bottom right:* Willem van de Poll, National Archives of the Netherlands
bottom left: Tel Aviv-Yafo Municipal Archives

p. 17 *top right:* Yaacov Ben Dov, Judaica Collection of the Harry Elkins Widener Memorial Library, Harvard University, Repository JPCDPZA55942

p. 18 *top right:* Oster Visual Documentation Center, ANU-Museum of the Jewish People
bottom left: by kind permission of the Tel-Aviv Encyclopedia, www.tlv100.net

p.19 *top right:* digitized from the Howard J. Swibel Library Preservation Fund in the Harvard College Library (Fund 560435)

p. 20 *bottom left:* Zoltan Kluger, GPO National Photo Collection

p. 21 *top right:* Tel Aviv-Yafo Municipal Archives
bottom right: unknown photographer, GPO National Photo Collection

p. 22 *bottom right:* Rudi Weissenstein, The PhotoHouse Collection

p. 24 *top right:* Avraham Soskin, Soskin Collection, MUSA, Eretz Israel Museum, Tel Aviv
bottom right: Yael Rozen

p. 25 *top right:* Central Zionist Archives

p. 26 *bottom left:* Zoltan Kluger, GPO National Photo Collection

p. 27 *top right:* unknown photographer, GPO National Photo Collection
bottom right: Matson Photo Service, G. Eric and Edith Matson Photograph Collection, Library of Congress Prints and Photographs Division, Washington, DC, https://www.loc.gov/item/mpc2005009102/PP/

p. 30 *bottom left:* Mori Rader, Tel Aviv-Yafo Municipal Archives, by kind permission of Rachel Rader

p. 31 *top right:* Moshe Milner, GPO National Photo Collection

p. 32 *top left:* unknown photographer
bottom left: Fritz Cohen, GPO National Photo Collection

p. 33 *top right:* Fritz Cohen, GPO National Photo Collection

p. 34 *top right:* unknown photographer, GPO National Photo Collection
bottom left: Willem van de Poll, National Archives of the Netherlands

p. 35 *top right:* unknown photographer, GPO National Photo Collection

p. 36 *bottom left:* Oskar Krockenberger, Shay Farkash Collection

p. 37 *top right:* Beno Rothenberg photo collection, Israel State Archive

p. 38 *top right:* Historic Collection/Alamy Stock Photo

p. 39 *top right:* scan from *The New Standard Jewish Encyclopedia* by Geoffrey Wigoder, Wikimedia Commons, https://commons.wikimedia.org/wiki/File:Abraham_Mapu.jpg

p. 40 *bottom right:* Tel Aviv-Yafo Municipal Archives
bottom left: Fritz Cohen, GPO National Photo Collection

p. 41 *top right:* Zoltan Kluger, GPO National Photo Collection

p. 42 *bottom left:* Willem van de Poll, National Archives of the Netherlands

p. 43 *top left:* Rudolph Yonas, Central Zionist Archives
top right: Central Zionist Archives

p. 44 *top right:* Courtesy of Beit Ha'ir, Tel Aviv-Yafo Municipality, Tel Aviv Revealed to the Eye, Gustav Rubinstein collection, by kind permission of his son, Adam Rubinstein
bottom right: Central Zionist Archives

p. 45 *top right:* The Pritzker Family National Photography Collection, Abraham Schwadron Collection, The National Library of Israel

p. 46 *top right:* Itzhak Amit, Judaica Collection of the Harry Elkins Widener Memorial Library, Harvard University

p. 47 *top right:* Israel State Archive, Yehudah Eisenstark photo collection

p. 48 *bottom left:* WIZO Archives

p. 49 *top right:* Central Zionist Archives

p. 50 *bottom left:* Central Zionist Archives

p. 51 *top left:* Central Zionist Archives
top right: from a postcard published by the Jewish National Fund, featuring a portrait of Henrietta Szold by photographer Alexander Ganen, 1940

p. 52 *bottom left:* Zoltan Kluger, GPO National Photo Collection

p. 53 *top right:* unknown photographer, GPO National Photo Collection

p. 54 *top right:* Dalia Levi-Eliyahu postcards collection, Eliyahu Bros
bottom right: Avraham Soskin, Soskin Collection, MUSA, Eretz Israel Museum, Tel Aviv

p. 55 *top right:* AZ Project, Tel-Hai Museum

p. 56 *bottom right:* Oster Visual Documentation Center, ANU-Museum of the Jewish People, courtesy of Chaya Galai, Tel Aviv
bottom left: courtesy of Yad Chaim Weizmann, The Weizmann Archives, Rehovot, Israel

p. 57 *top right:* Central Zionist Archives

p. 60 *top right:* Avraham Soskin, Soskin Collection, MUSA, Eretz Israel Museum, Tel Aviv
bottom right: Dalia Levi-Eliyahu postcards collection, Eliyahu Bros

p. 61 *top right:* The Pritzker Family National Photography Collection, Abraham Schwadron Collection, The National Library of Israel

p. 62 *top right:* cover of A. Z. Ben-Jischai, *Tel Aviv* [in German] (Jerusalem: Keren Hayesod, 1936)

p. 63 *top left:* Central Zionist Archives
top right: World History Archive/Alamy Stock Photo

p. 64 *top right:* Central Zionist Archives
bottom right: Zehavi Collection ,Yad Ben-Zvi Photo Archives

p. 65 *top right:* Grantham Bain Collection, Library of Congress Prints and Photographs Division, Washington, DC

p. 66 *bottom right:* Dalia Levi-Eliyahu postcards collection, Eliyahu Bros

p. 67 *top right:* Shlomo Narinsky, The Pritzker Family National Photography Collection, Abraham Schwadron Collection, The National Library of Israel

p. 68 *bottom right:* Dalia Levi-Eliyahu postcards collection, Eliyahu Bros
bottom left: G. Eric and Edith Matson Photograph Collection, Library of Congress Prints and Photographs Division, Washington, DC, https://hdl.loc.gov/loc.pnp/res.258.mats

p. 69 *top right:* The Pritzker Family National Photography Collection, Abraham Schwadron Collection, The National Library of Israel

p. 70 *top right:* Dalia Levi-Eliyahu postcards collection, Eliyahu Bros *bottom left:* Dalia Levi-Eliyahu postcards collection, Eliyahu Bros

p. 71 *top right:* The Pritzker Family National Photography Collection, Abraham Schwadron Collection, The National Library of Israel

p. 72 *top right:* Matson Photo Service, G. Eric and Edith Matson Photograph Collection, Library of Congress Prints and Photographs Division, Washington, DC, www.loc.gov/item/2019704415
bottom left: KKL-JNF Photo Archive

p. 73 *top left:* unknown photographer, GPO National Photo Collection
top right: KKL-JNF Photo Archive

p. 75 *bottom left:* Central Zionist Archives

p. 76 *top right:* Matson Photo Service, G. Eric and Edith Matson Photograph Collection, Library of Congress Prints and Photographs Division, Washington, DC, www.loc.gov/item/2019703937/

p. 77 *top right:* The Pritzker Family National Photography Collection, Abraham Schwadron Collection, The National Library of Israel

p. 78 *bottom right:* unknown photographer

p. 79 *top left:* Moshe Milner, GPO National Photo Collection
top right: unknown photographer, GPO National Photo Collection

p. 82 *right:* Willem van de Poll, National Archives of the Netherlands

p. 83 *top left:* Yaacov Rozner, KKL-JNF Photo Archive
top right: The Pritzker Family National Photography Collection, Abraham Schwadron Collection, The National Library of Israel

p. 84 *bottom left:* Tel Aviv-Yafo Municipal Archives

p. 85 *top right:* Central Zionist Archives

p. 86 *bottom right:* Rudi Weissenstein, The PhotoHouse Collection

p. 87 *top left:* Rachel Hirsch
top right: The Pritzker Family National Photography Collection, Abraham Schwadron Collection, The National Library of Israel

p. 88 *bottom right:* Nati Harnik, GPO National Photo Collection
bottom left: Moshe Milner, GPO National Photo Collection

p. 89 *top right:* Yaacov Saar, GPO National Photo Collection

p. 90 *right:* Zoltan Kluger, GPO National Photo Collection
bottom left: Yaacov Rozner, KKL-JNF Photo Archive

p. 91 *top right:* The Pritzker Family National Photography Collection, Abraham Schwadron Collection, The National Library of Israel

p. 94 *top right:* Rachel Hirsch
bottom right: Zvi Oron, Central Zionist Archives

p. 95 *top right:* courtesy of Or Aleksandrowicz

p. 96 *bottom right:* Ora Sapir, Eitin Family Collection
bottom left: Ora Sapir, Eitin Family Collection

p. 97 *top right:* The Pritzker Family National Photography Collection, Abraham Schwadron collection, The National Library of Israel

p. 98 *top right:* Central Zionist Archives
bottom right: postcard published by Moshe Ardman

p. 99 *top right:* Bitmuna Collections, Miriam and Lev Klotz Collection, The Pritzker Family National Photography Collection, National Library of Israel

p. 100 *bottom right:* Rudi Weissenstein, The PhotoHouse Collection
bottom left: photographer unknown

p. 102 *bottom right:* Yisra'el Simionski/Israel Sun Ltd., Judaica Collection of the Harry Elkins Widener Memorial Library, Harvard University
bottom left: Kurt Bremmer Collection, by kind permission of Rannan Bremmer and Henya Melichson

p. 106 *top right:* Dalia Levi-Eliyahu postcards collection, Eliyahu Bros
bottom right: Yoel Amir Collection

p. 107 *top right:* The Pritzker Family National Photography Collection, Abraham Schwadron Collection, The National Library of Israel

p. 108 *bottom:* Israel State Archive

p. 109 *top right:* The Pritzker Family National Photography Collection, The National Library of Israel, Abraham Schwadron collection

p. 110 *bottom right:* unknown photographer, GPO National Photo Collection
bottom left: Frank Scholten collection, The Netherlands Institute for the Near East, Leiden

p. 111 *top right:* unknown photographer, GPO National Photo Collection

p. 114 *bottom right:* Willie Folander, Tel Aviv-Yafo Municipal Archives

p. 115 *top right:* unknown photographer, GPO National Photo Collection

p. 116 *top right:* Zoltan Kluger, GPO National Photo Collection